THROUGH THE EYES OF THE BAY COLONY

The Story of the Involvement of Massachusetts-Bay in the Battle of Ticonderoga

1758

Brenton C. Kemmer

HERITAGE BOOKS
2008

HERITAGE BOOKS

AN IMPRINT OF HERITAGE BOOKS, INC.

Books, CDs, and more—Worldwide

For our listing of thousands of titles see our website
at
www.HeritageBooks.com

Published 2008 by
HERITAGE BOOKS, INC.
Publishing Division
100 Railroad Ave. #104
Westminster, Maryland 21157

Other books by Brenton C. Kemmer:

Redcoats, Yankees, and Allies:
A History of Uniforms, Clothing, and Gear of the British Army
in the Lake George-Lake Champlain Corridor, 1755-1760

Freemen, Freeholders and Citizen Soldiers:
An Organizational History of Colonel Jonathan Bagley's Regiment, 1755-1760

So, Ye Want to be a Reenactor? A Living History Handbook
Brenton C. Kemmer and Karen L. Kemmer

War, Hell and Honor: A Novel of the French and Indian War

The Partisans: Second in a Series of Novels of the French and Indian War

Capture and Redemption: Third in a Series of Novels of the French and Indian War

International Standard Book Numbers
Paperbound: 978-0-7884-4675-7
Clothbound: 978-0-7884-7226-8

CONTENTS

ACKNOWLEDGMENTS

I have been a rarity in many people's eyes, enjoying history since I was a child. In my adult life I have been very lucky to be employed in the study and education of history. I have as well, been blessed, being able to incorporate history as my hobby. To some, this must seem strange, but to others wonderment. To me, it is shear pleasure.

In the 1990's, I was working on my graduate program and was fortunate to have the opportunity to take several research trips to upper state New York with several other educators and university students. We were on a quest to see as many of the original sites that still existed over our spring breaks. We were lucky that one person in the group had been to New York several times and was able to connect us with knowledgeable persons and take us to many of the sites where the French and Indian War took place. A few of these sites still exist today, but for many the location is all that is known by a few. Some of these sites included: Fort Miller, Fort Edward, Rogers' Island, Halfway Brook Post, Fort William Henry, Fort George, Fort Gage, Fort William, Fort Ticonderoga, Fort Crown Point, Fort Ste. Frederic, Fort Anne, Bloody Pond, Bloody Morning Scout, Rogers' Rock and South Bay.

It was on these trips that I met two men that helped me in my early research and the finding of some of these sites. One was a man who at that time owned Rogers' Island. Earl Stott was a very eccentric man who had been intimate with the historic sites of Lake George all his life. He had grown up and cut his teeth at Ticonderoga. Earl, with the proper archaeological training, would have been one of the forerunners in tangible artifacts dealing with the French and Indian War in the Lake George / Hudson River area.

The second man, a fellow Midwesterner, Nick Westbrook, was introduced to me his first year as director at Fort Ticonderoga. He invited us to his home and took us into areas of the fort that were astounding. Nick has always been willing to go that extra mile in assisting my research or pointing me to others in the Fort's staff with particular expertise. Nick was extremely supportive of my earlier works with my publisher and was generous with the assistance of the fort and its resources.

Without people like these men and the ability of walking the ground that these soldiers had, a true writer only speculates on his content. One must go that extra mile: not just read their diaries, journals and letter, not just look at the artifacts they left behind, not just look at their cartography of the period. One must go to the actual area and be where they have been. For this, I am truly thankful.

Enjoy the retelling of this monumental battle, The Battle of Ticonderoga, told THROUGH THE EYES OF THE BAY COLONY.

Cover photo by: Ronald Casto

TICONDEROGA

From the formation of Massachusetts-Bay Colony, settlers had transplanted their European culture that bore the names of so many of their English hamlets, towns and countries. One of the rudimentary aspects of these founding fathers was their well-established militarism. Their arms and armor, banners and traditions began in the early 1600's to give Massachusetts-Bay, also known as the Bay Colony, personality.

For several generations, the military, religious and social heritage of these colonists, along with the expansion and colonization, transformed Massachusetts-Bay's character. The 1750's, however, brought about a culmination of tensions between the two superpowers of the eighteenth century. France and her Canadian colonists, along with their Native Allies, would be forced to do battle against England and her thirteen North American colonies. This war would take place on the natural stage of a great waterway linking North America in all four cardinal directions: Lake George / Lake Champlain Corridor.

This thoroughfare of lakes, rivers and mountains formed the fastest means of communication and travel between Canada and the middle and eastern United States for centuries. Geologically, the mountains known today as the Adirondacks create the southern most portion of the Canadian Shield. This ancient landform consists primarily of metamorphic rock: rock that has transformed or changed under great pressure or heat, producing great physical or even chemical change.

Part of the pressure forced on the rock masses uplifted the shield forming the Adirondack Mountains. Further changes via faults and glacial erosion shaped the mountains as they look today. These same glaciations further changed the lands between the St. Lawrence and the Hudson Rivers, forming the thousands of lakes and rivers used by Aboriginal peoples and eventually Europeans of the eighteenth century. Some of these lakes and rivers include Lake George, Lake Champlain, and the Hudson, Mohawk, and St. Lawrence Rivers.

This natural water route etched within the Adirondacks was first used by the northeastern Aborigines for thousands of years prior to European exploration. Not only was this the main mode of transportation, but also a vibrant habitat brimming with fish, fowl and game to subsist the earliest hunters and gatherers had formed. As these early hunters and gatherers developed semi-permanent villages for the growing of their main stay, maize, they continued to reap the wealth of the Adirondacks for hunting and fishing as well as developing superb trade routes.

With the colonization of North America, the Adirondack area became split. This region was shared with the Mohawks and the Five Nations of the Iroquois living to the west, while the Abenaki lived in the northeast and the Mahicans in the southeast.

In 1609, two European nations established their destinies in the Adirondack region. French explorer Samuel de Champlain ventured south from Quebec with sixty Huron and Montagnais warriors and three fellow Frenchmen. This party was looking for Iroquois enemies to battle. Near the southern end of the lake that eventually bore his name, Champlain and his party met with a superior force of Iroquois and fought on the peninsula of Ticonderoga. Champlain and his fellow Frenchmen's harquebuses (black powder weapons) proved superior to the Iroquois' greater numbers. Several weeks later, Englishman Henry Hudson was less than one hundred miles south of Ticonderoga exploring and claiming lands along the river that would be named after him.

The first white military expedition traveling through the Ticonderoga area was a French raiding party in 1661. Then in 1671, a British raiding party traversed the peninsula. It was not until 1731 that a fortified tower was built by the French at Crown Point, only about twelve miles north of Ticonderoga. By this time, the English had advanced their settlements and forts as far north as Saratoga, which they called Schuylerville. This placed the two superpowers only sixty miles apart.

Surprisingly, until the 1750's little fighting took place on or around Ticonderoga, despite Queen Anne's and King George's Wars. Several small fortified outposts were built, shortening the distance between the two enemies. A stockade fur post was built by John Henry Lydius on the eastern bank of the Hudson River. Another was a blockhouse and stockade called Fort Anne near

Wood Creek, north of the Hudson and east of Lake George (called Lake St. Sacrament by the French).

In 1755, the distance between French and British forts shortened to only thirty miles. William Johnson, of New York Colony, headed north with an all-provincial army, the largest contingent from Massachusetts-Bay. His orders as the commander were to destroy Crown Point and secure the area for the British Crown. He moved his army to the fur post built by Lydius and began construction of a much larger fortification. This fort was named Fort Edward and would be the largest group of buildings and largest defensive post north of Albany. Then Johnson moved up to the lake that he named Lake George. Before any fortifications could be built on the lake, Johnson's camp was attacked by the French and their Indians. Johnson's provincial army prevailed, and his army then began to build Fort William Henry adjacent to his camp.

The French army headed back north to their camp on the peninsula of Ticonderoga. On September 20, 1755 the French Canadian Governor gave orders to Sieur de Lotbiniere, a young engineer, to build a fort. Later that month, British scouts reported that the peninsula had about 3,000 soldiers encamped and a foundation started for a fort. By December, word came that the French had four barracks buildings within the walls and close to two dozen huts outside. The French named the fort Carillon.

There was a continuous building on the two forts for the next year and a half. The only military action seen were skirmishes until July, 1757, when the Marquis de Montcalm lead a French army to the south shore of Lake George, laid siege to and captured Fort William Henry. Montcalm had Fort William Henry destroyed and returned his army to Carillon, where they continued to strengthen their fort. The British continued work at Fort Edward, and in the spring of 1758 the British and French were poised for another major siege. This time, the offense was lead by King George's army against Fort Carillon.

OF LOG AND STONE, IN THE WILDERNESS

The Marquis de Vaudreuil, Governor General of New France, saw the importance of moving south of Fort Ste. Frederic to Crown Point and raising a new fortification near the falls and portage between the two great lakes, Lake George and Lake Champlain. Vaudreuil ordered the young engineer, Sieur de Lotbiniere, to oversee construction. In September and October of 1755, Vaudreuil ordered land to be laid out for a stone fort on the forested peninsula of Ticonderoga. Work began with the clearing of the old growth trees and the leveling of the rocky terrain.

The young engineer had been educated in the methods of fortification that were perfected by the great Marshal Vauban. Using the geometry of fortification, Lotbiniere eventually designed Carillon into a formidable star-shaped stone fort. Bastions with thick ramparts walled Carillon and provided crossfire from the fort's cannons. Demilunes and a glacis eventually defended two of her walls as well.

Lotbiniere soon realized that he did not have the workmen or materials to build the fort out of stone, so he resorted to a much less skilled construction. The fort walls were made of two rows of large oak logs. Ten feet separated the inner and outer walls, which were held together by dovetailed cross pieces. The space between was filled with dirt, rubble and mud. By November 28, the walls were seven feet high. One of Lotbiniere's greatest concerns was shelter for a sizable garrison. He had cleared an area large enough for a camp of 3,000 troops in front of the fort. By his departure in February, 1756, there were four barracks buildings inside the fort and nearly two dozen huts and other buildings outside. There were also twelve cannons in place.

Lotbiniere returned to Carillon in May, 1756. That summer contained much partisan warfare but little large scale battles in the area near Carillon. Building continued and the walls rose higher. Earthen ramparts and platforms for the bastions were completed. A cover was built for each bastion bomb-proof. A large blockhouse was constructed at the southeast corner of the fort.

After the peninsula was cleared more, Lotbiniere realized that the fort was not in the optimum place on the peninsula. In order to make up for this oversight, a redoubt of log and earth, called the Grenadier's Battery, was constructed on the point of the peninsula to command the narrows of the lake.

To assist in materials for construction, a lime kiln and brickworks were built. A sawmill was built but was not used at the lower falls of the La Chute River. There was no experienced millwright in the garrison.

Two stone barracks and a hospital were under construction. Just outside the southern gate, a large log storehouse was built. This was a square shaped structure used as a ravelin. Cannons were placed on its roof. Now the fort mounted a minimum of thirty cannons. Ditches were dug as well as two demilunes as deep as the bedrock, which was shallow on this peninsula.[10] Louis Antoine de Bougainville, the aid-de-camp to the Marquis de Montcalm commander of the French army in North America, wrote a good description of Carillon that he published in his journal dating September 11, 1756.

> "Fort Carillon, commenced last fall, is situated almost at the head of Lake Champlain on a peninsula pointing south which divides the lake from the south bay, and to the north the outlet of Lake George. The fort is square with four bastions of which three are in a defensible state. It is of horizontal timbers. The position is well chosen on a rugged rock formation, but the fort is badly oriented and is not far enough out on the north point of the lake, which has obliged them to make a redoubt at the place where the fort should have been. As for

---

[10] Hamilton, Edward, P. *Fort Ticonderoga, Key To A* Continent, *With An Introduction By Nicholas Westbrook* (Ticonderoga, N.Y.:   Fort Ticonderoga Museum, 1995) 41-43 & 48-49; Pell, S.H.P. *Fort Ticonderoga, A Short History* (Ticonderoga, N.Y.: Fort Ticonderoga Museum, 1987) 19 & 25; *Reminiscences of the French War, Robert Rogers' Journal and a Memoir of General Stark.* Freedom, N. H.: The Freedom Historical Society, 1988, 24-25; "The Building Of The Fort," *The Bulletin of the Fort Ticonderoga Museum* 2 #3 (January 1931): 88-92.

the rest of it they would have done better to take advantage of the rock, breaking it up with a pickaxe and using it for the parapets.

The camp is on the river's edge at the foot of the rocky formation. It is presently composed of the battalions of La Reine, Languedoc, Royal Roussellon, and some colony troops. Guyenne and Bearn are camped half a league away at the Falls of Lake St. Sacrament."[11]

The year 1757 saw a change in warfare for the Lake George / Lake Champlain Corridor. That summer saw a major siege by the French army garrisoned at Carillon upon the British army at Fort William Henry. The French commanding general, the Marquis de Montcalm, sallied south, laid siege to British Fort William Henry and successfully defeated its garrison and destroyed the fort.

The French army, upon returning to Fort Carillon, continued construction. Now there were thirty-six cannons in place and one third were eighteen pounders. The French had fortified the area near the falls on the east shore of Lake George by building a blockhouse. The major change now was that the artificers and laborers began to replace the timbered walls of Fort Carillon with stone, making the fort more defensible against cannon.[12]

---

[11] Hamilton, Edward P. *Adventure In The Wilderness, The American Journals of Louis Antoine de Bougainville, 1756-1760* (London: University of Oklahoma Press) 33-34.
[12] Bulletin, 93; Hamilton, *Fort Ticonderoga*, 49; Pell, 20 & 25; Rogers, 43-44.

THE BAY-COLONY

MARCHES FORTH

Calling on the "Freeborn Englishmen" of the Bay-Colony, the General Court of Massachusetts gave orders to raise eight regiments. These regiments were sent forth under General Abercrombie's Crown Point expedition to drive the French and their allied Indians from the Lake George / Lake Champlain waterway. The eight Colonels, commissioned regimental commanders, were Timothy Ruggles, Jedidiah Preble, Jonathan Bagley, Thomas Doty, Ebenezer Nichols, William Williams, Joseph Williams and Oliver Partridge.

Documentation on most of these gentlemen is numerous, but a few have almost been lost to the ages. To help set the tone for the command of the players in this epic campaign, a short biography of each Colonel of the Bay-Colony in 1758 can be found below.

Timothy Ruggles was born in 1711 in Rochester, Massachusetts. His father was the Reverend Timothy Ruggles. Colonel Ruggles graduated from Harvard in 1732.

Upon graduating, Ruggles began a law practice that year in Rochester. In 1737, he moved his practice to Sandwich, Massachusetts and in 1753 to Hardwick, Massachusetts. In 1757, Ruggles became a judge of the Court of Common-Men Pleas of Worcester County. He also opened a tavern in Sandwich, and it has been said that Ruggles tended the bar and the stables himself.

Ruggles began his public service in 1736, having been elected to the Massachusetts House of Representatives where he served for thirty years. In 1755, he was commissioned Colonel of a regiment serving on the Crown Point Expedition lead by General William Johnson. He took part in the famed Battle of Lake George.

He continued as a regimental Colonel for the next three years in the same theater of operations.[3]

Colonel Jedidiah Preble was born in York, Massachusetts (now Maine) in 1707. In 1748, he took up residence in Falmouth, Massachusetts (now Portland, Maine).

Preble served his colony as a councilor, judge and representative. Also, he was a large landowner and shipping businessman.

The Colonel's military career began with the 1745 Siege of Louisbourg. This is when he was promoted to Captain. During the 1755 Expedition and the Removal of the French Acadian's, Preble served as Lieutenant Colonel in Colonel Winslow's Regiment. In 1758, Preble was commissioned Colonel of his own regiment.[4]

Jonathan Bagley was born in Amesbury in 1717. He began as a husbandman. He acquired large landholdings, several wafts along the Pow Wow and Merrimac Rivers, and owned a gristmill, saw mill, lumber business, and lime kiln.

Bagley served eleven terms in the Massachusetts House, beginning in 1743.

By 1743, he was a Lieutenant in the militia, and in 1746 he was Captain of the fifth company of the fifth Regiment under Colonel Robert Hale. This service was during the Louisbourg Campaign. In 1755, Bagley was Lieutenant Colonel of Colonel Moses Titcomb's Regiment serving at the Battle of Lake George. Titcomb was killed in this battle, and Bagley was promoted to Colonel of the regiment. He remained at Lake George that winter and helped oversee much of the building of Fort William Henry. He was commandant of Fort Edward and Fort William Henry that winter. Bagley continued service as a regimental Colonel for Massachusetts through 1756, 1757 and 1758.[5]

---

[3] Massachusetts Officers in the French and Indian Wars, 1748-1763, The Society of Colonial Wars, ed. Nancy S. Voye (Boston: The New England Historic Genealogical Society, 1975; http://en.wikipedia.org/wiki/Timothy Ruggles; http://famousamericans.net/timothyruggles/

[4] Voye; http://www.surnameguide.com/preble/abraham_preble_genealogy.htm.

[5] Amesbury Public Library Archives, "Bagley Family History," Amesbury Public Library, Amesbury, Massachusetts, Donated by Leonard Johnson, Sept. 1968, p. 24-31; Brenton C. Kemmer, *Freemen, Freeholders, and Citizen Soldiers, an*

Thomas Doty was one of those men who were somewhat lost to history. However, some facts are known about his life. He was from Plymouth, Massachusetts. In 1755, he served as Major in Colonel Joseph Thacher's Regiment, and in 1756 he was Lieutenant Colonel in the same regiment. It appears he did not serve in 1757, but in 1758 he was Colonel of his own regiment heading toward Lake George.[6]

Ebenezer Nichols was born in 1703 in Reading, Massachusetts. Nichols served his colony in many capacities such as selectman, justice of the peace and representative. He was commissioned a Colonel in 1756 and again in 1758 through February, 1759.[7]

William Williams was born in Weston, Massachusetts in 1713. He graduated from Harvard in 1729 as number eleven out of twenty-eight. Early on, Williams had a business career in Boston. He moved to Pontoosuck (now Pittsfield, Massachusetts) in 1753-54. He became known as the patriarch of Pontoosuck because of his prominence in the community. Wanting to change his career, Colonel Williams served as a surgeon in 1739. By 1741, Williams was commissioned an Ensign for an expedition to the West Indies. Around 1743, he moved to Deerfield, Massachusetts and was Lieutenant Colonel in the Northern Hampshire regiment. In 1744, he was placed in charge of building Fort Shirley in western Massachusetts. In 1747, he was placed in charge of the rebuilding of Fort Massachusetts, also in far western Massachusetts. He was commissioned Captain in 1748 and continued serving as such in 1754-1755. In 1758, he was given command of one of the eight

---

Organizational History of Colonel Jonathan Bagley's Regiment 1755-1760 (Bowie, MD.: Heritage Books, Inc., 1997) 6-7; Martha Anderson and Norton Bagley, " Some Descendants of Orlando Bagley of Amesbury, Massachusetts," Genealogical Society of the Church of Jesus Christ of Latter-Day Saints (microfilm, 1973) 1: 5-6, 14-16, 34-36; Fred Anderson, to Brenton C. Kemmer, 1994, Massachusetts Archival Records for Bagley Family, Author's Private Collections, Houghton Lake, Michigan.

[6] Voye; http://www.stoughtonhistory.com/dotytavern.htm

[7] Voye: http://clarku.edu/search.cfm?query=ebenezer&start=610&max=10

Massachusetts Regiments and served till February, 1759. William Williams then retired on half-pay.[8]

Colonel Joseph Williams was born at Roxbury, Massachusetts in 1709. It was said that he was a very eccentric man. He seems to have only served for the 1758 campaign. His regiment did not serve in the 1758 Ticonderoga assault but rather was stationed in the Mohawk Valley at Fort Herkimer and the Great Carrying Place, also called Fort Stanwix.[9]

Oliver Partridge was born in Hatfield, Massachusetts in 1712. He graduated from Yale College in 1730, second out of a class of eighteen, where he studied surveying. Partridge acted as High County Sheriff. In 1734, he married into the most prominent family in western Massachusetts, the Williams family. Partridge was a well landed gentleman who served his colony on the Court of Common Pleas in Hampshire County, served on the Committee for Defense planning the line of western forts and was representative for the Albany Congress of 1754.

He served as Lieutenant Colonel of the militia from 1755-57 and served at Fort Massachusetts. This regiment was Colonel Israel Williams' Regiment of western forces. Partridge became Colonel of this regiment in 1757. Partridge was usually on "ranger service." He was also the local Muster Master, recruiting for the Bay Colony Regiments. Oliver Partridge commanded a unique unit during the 1758 campaign. His unit, a battalion, was called by three names: Partridge's Rangers, Partridge's Light Infantry, and The Royal Hunters.

The commander of the 1758 campaign against Ticonderoga, General James Abercrombie, gave a good insight to Partridge's character.

---

[8] Arthur L. Perry, *Origins in Williamstown* (New York: Charles Scribner's Sons, 1894), 247; Michael D. Coe, *The Line of Forts, Historical Archaeology on the Colonial Frontier of Massachusetts* (Lebanon, NH.: University Press of New England, 2006) 193; "The American Quarterly Register," (Boston: Harvard, Edwards, B.B. and Cogswell, W.) 13 (1841) 405, www.books.google.com; Holland, Josiah Gilbert, *History of Western* Massachusetts (Springfield: Samuel Bowles and Company, 1855), 548, www.book.google.com; Voye;
[9] "New England Historical and Genealogical," (H.F. Waters) 37-52 (1883-98) 339, www.books.google.com; Voye.

"The Govr. Of the Massachusetts Bay last letter to me is of the 7th Instant, by which he acquaints me that he will issue Orders to the Regiments to March;... He further tells me, that tho' the General Assembly made Provision for Seven Regiments only, yet out of the 7000, he has formed a Battalion of light Infantry or Rangers, to consist of 500 Men, to be commanded by Colonel Oliver Partridge, one of the very first Men of that Country, whose Character, & the Service he may be of to me, in dealing with their People, he will make me acquainted with."[10]

Copies of fifteen diaries and journals of Massachusetts's soldiers who marched from their colony to New York in 1758 have been accumulated. These give an ample cross section of the men from four regiments from this colony. Of these primary documents five are officers, one a surgeon and one a chaplain leaving eight enlisted men. One soldier also shipped out early with a unit of carpenters several months prior to the other regiments marching. Below is a listing of the soldiers, where they hailed from and which Massachusetts Regiment they belonged to.

Captain. Samuel Cobb, Middleboro, MA., Colonel Preble's Regiment
Captain William Sweat, Salisbury, MA., Colonel Preble's Regiment
Private Elijah Estabrook, Haverhill, MA., Colonel Preble's Regiment
Anonymous diary, Colonel Preble's Regiment

---

[10] Coe, 186; De Forest, Louis Effingham ed. The Journals and Papers of Seth Pomeroy. The Society of Colonial Wars. New Haven, Conn.: The Turtle Morehouse and Taylor Co., 1926"The Correspondence of William Pitt When Secretary of State, with Colonial Governors and Military and Naval Commissioners in America," The MacMillan Company, London & New York, 1906; reprinted by the Kraus Reprint Co., New York, 1969. Letter from James Abercromby to William Pitt, from Albany, May 22, 1758; *Origins in Williamstown*, 225-226, 274, 292, 297, 298, 335; Voye.

Captain Asa Foster, Andover, MA., Colonel Nichols' Regiment
Private Joseph Holt, Andover, MA., Colonel Nichols' Regiment
Private Amos Richardson, Woburn, MA., Colonel Nichols' Regiment

Dr. Caleb Rea, Danvers, MA., Colonel Bagley's Regiment
Reverend John Cleaveland, Ipswich, MA., Colonel Bagley's Regiment
Private Archelaus Fuller, Middleton, MA., Colonel Bagley's Regiment
Private John Noyes, Newbury, MA., Colonel Bagley's Regiment

Lieutenant Benjamin Bass, Colonel Joseph Williams' Regiment
Ensign Moses Dorr, Roxbury, MA., Colonel Joseph Williams' Regiment

Private Benjamin Glasier, Ipswich, MA., unit of carpenters

In February, a 1758 Militia Act was published by the Massachusetts Colony setting forth measures for the trainbands (militias). It dictated the second and third Mondays of April for all men, sixteen to sixty years old, to muster with arms and amunition.[11] Consequently, the colonels and colony had been commissioning officers to recruit soldiers for the Massachusetts Regiments in early April, which is documented by Lieutenant John Hawks' beating orders dating April 10, 1758.[12] By April 4, the day after the first April muster of 1758, John Noyes received an

---

[11] Armand F. Lucier *French and Indian War Notices, Abstracted from Colonial Newspapers* (Bowie, MD.: Heritage Books, Inc. 1999) vol. 3, p. 17-22; Brenton C. Kemmer, 2007, Facsimile Reproduction "Militia Act, 1758, Massachusetts-Bay, February 13, 1758, Author's Private Collections, Houghton Lake, Michigan.
[12] Library of Congress, 12/22/07,
http://memory.loc.gov/rbc/rbpe/rbpe03/rbpe035/0350230a/001dq.gif

enlistment bounty for recruiting into Colonel Jonathan Bagley's Regiment.[13] For the next month, soldiers and officers recruited received bounties, and some officers, like Captain William Sweat, were commissioned as late as early May. It was the intent of the British government to repay the colonies for generous enlistment bounties for this campaign.[14]

With the exception of part of Colonel Preble's Regiment, the Massachusetts men marched to Lake George from their homes. Beginning May 21, 1758, Captain Samuel Cobb chronicled sailing on transports from Winter Harbor, Maine with five and one half companies of Preble's Regiment. These men sailed on seven transports landing at Kittery, Grayhead and on through Hell's Gates to Long Island Sound, New York. From the Sound, they sailed up the Hudson River on June 1, 1758. They had joined the rest of the Bay Colony at Albany, New York on June 7.[15]

The vast majority of the soldiery of the Bay Colony took a common line of march. Most were on the march, departing homes between May 21 and May 29, 1758. This meant that the roads were congested with detachments and companies of soldiers marching toward New York Colony.[16]

Each man was allotted billeting money, money for his subsistence along the march. Inns were the most common stop over facilities of the colonial period for shelter and food. Periodically

---

[13] Journal of John Noyes of Newbury (Salem: Essex Institute, Historical Collections) vol. 45 (1909) 73.
[14] Captain William Sweat's Personal Diary of the Expedition Against Ticonderoga, May 2 – November 7, 1758 (Salem: Essex Institute, Historical Collections) vol. VCIII (1957) 36.
[15] "The Journal of Captain Samuel Cobb, May 21, 1758-October 29, 1758," Fort Ticonderoga Museum, Bulletin 14 (1981): 15.
[16] "Amos Richardson's Journal, 1758," The Bulletin of the Fort Ticonderoga Museum vol. 12 (1968): 269; "Archelaus Fuller's Journal, 1758," The Bulletin of the Fort Ticonderoga Museum vol. 13 (1970): 6; Brenton C. Kemmer, 2007, photo copy "A Journal of an Expedition Against Canada by Moses Dorr Ensign of Captain Parkers Company, Roxbury, May 25th, 1758," Author's Private Collections, Houghton Lake, MI., p. 452; F. M. Ray, ed., The Journal of Dr. Caleb Rea (Salem: Privately Printed, 1881), 87; Hal Skaarup, transcription to Brenton C. Kemmer 2000, "Journal of Elijah Estabrooks, 1758-59-60," Author's Private Collection, Houghton Lake, MI., May 21, 1758; "Journal of Joseph Holt, of Wilton, N.H. in the Canada Expedition of 1758," New England Historical and Genealogical Register 10 (1856) 307; Journal of John Noyes of Newbury (Salem: Essex Institute, Historical Collections) vol. 45 (1909) 73; Sweat, 36.

they were so full that men were lodged in meetinghouses, barns and other buildings. Below is a list of many of the Inns frequented by Bay Colony soldiers on their march.

Name of Inn:		Location in Massachusetts:
Moses Bayle Inn	-	Newbury
Webster's Inn	-	Haverhill
Henry Abit Inn	-	Andover
Kiteridge Inn	-	Tewksburg
Benjamin Lewis Inn	-	Billerica
Deacon Rice Inn	-	Suesburg
Colonel Williams' Inn	-	Marlboro
Stephen How Inn	-	Marlboro
Hobard Inn	-	Northampton
Amos Taylor Inn	-	Spencer
Nathan Wallcute Inn	-	Brookfield
Feniase Walker Inn	-	Brookfield
Buchminster Inn	-	Brookfield
Gillbord Inn	-	Newcom
John Downing Inn	-	River Parrish
Aron Dewit Inn	-	-
Nathanel Lyman Inn	-	-
Jonathan Graves Inn	-	-
Stern Inn	-	Worcester
Hogeboom Inn	-	Claveruck

As men of the Bay Colony converged from the north, south and east, they passed through many towns and eventually rendezvoused at Worcester, where part of the men received supplies, arms and accouterments. The soldiers marched west, following the main coach road past Brookfield and Cold Spring and arrived at Northampton on the Connecticut River. From this point west, the march was primarily through the woods, over hills and rivers and into the Berkshire Mountains. This part of the march was physically damaging and draining to most of the men.[17] This has been best told by Dr. Caleb Rea of Colonel Bagley's Regiment.

---

[17] Kemmer, Freemen, 53; Dorr, 453.

"This day arrived at Flat Bush Colonel Bagley's
Regiment, generally in good health and high spirits,
though some was very much beat out by their march
from Northampton, by the way of Pontoosuck to
Flat Bush, on which march many companies hadn't
one fourth allowance of bread nor any rum for four
or five days nor was there any to be had on ye road.
This scarcity of bread &c occasioned them to march
very fast so that many though difficulty of the way
got broken shins, sprained joints, bruised feet and
other accidental wounds by falling over stones and
stumps into quagmires &c and many by their over
heating and suddenly cooling was taken ye night
after their arrival at Flat Bush with pluralistic
symptoms, very few or none with the regular
symptoms of the camp fever. I can't remark here
the universal complaint there was among all ye Bay
Regiments of their being marched through the
woods by Pontoosuck, a way so had that it is
become a proverb, no one need pass muster or any
other proof of their fitness for a campaign but to
march through these woods."[18]

Within several days, the soldiers arrived at Fort Pontoosuck, also
called Williams' Fort. Here, more men received supplies as they
prepared once again to march into the woods and emerge at
Kinderhook on the Hudson River.

The soldiers now marched north on the great road past the
Halfway House, half way between Kinderhook and Albany. By
June 9 and 14, 1758, most of the Massachusetts Regiments had
assembled at Albany and were camped at the Flats or Greenbush.
Here, troops were fully equipped, accoutered and armed.[19]

On June 8, 1758, General Abercrombie gave orders for 300
Massachusetts men to march to Schenectady, New York. Colonel
Preble ordered three of his companies for this duty, one being

---

[18] Rea, 92-93.
[19] Cobb, 15; Dorr, 453; Esterbrooks June 8; Fuller, 7; Holt, 307; Rea, 90;
Richardson, 270; Sweat, 40.

Captain Cobb's. These men were issued their arms.[20] The other regiments between June 13 and June 19, 1758, were completed with their arms and ammunition. Men that had brought their own serviceable weapon were given a bounty on enlistment, but the vast majorities were at this time issued the King's arms or the Brown Bess musket at this time. This military weapon was the seventy-five caliber, smooth bore flintlock weapon that was used in differing forms by the British army from the beginning of the eighteenth century through the War of 1812.[21]

Other items issued to the Bay Colony troops came from the colony and not the King's stores. These soldiers were issued a blue woolen regimental coat faced in red along with woolen smallclothes (waistcoat or vest and breeches). They were also issued black tricorn hats with white ferreting (binding), shirts, hose and shoes. Many of these men also received knapsacks, blankets, hatchets and a wooden bottle or tin canteen.[22]

Upon arriving in Albany, all the Bay Colony Regiments were low on provisions. Consequently, they drew seven days rations. These foodstuffs amounted to meat, butter, rice and flour.[23]

The troops from Massachusetts, in general, did not tarry very long in the area of Albany. Within days of the other Bay Colony Regiments arriving, Glasier and the others in the detachment of carpenters marched north June 10, 1758.[24] Most Massachusetts troops averaged only a week at Albany before continuing toward Fort Edward.

Most of the soldiers trudged by foot; however, several record using whaleboats and bateaux to travel north. Captain Sweat stated on June 12, 1758, that they got two whaleboats to transport their baggage.[25]

Typically, the regiments marched from Greenbush or the Flats to Halfmoon, where they would cross the Hudson River. This distance was listed in diaries at approximately eight miles and took one day to march. Then the troops marched nine miles to Stillwater in one day. The next day they traveled fourteen miles, arriving at

[20] Cobb, 15.
[21] Fuller, 7-8; Richardson, 271.
[23] Estabrook, June 9; Fuller, 7; Holt, 307; Richardson, 270; Sweat, 40.
[24] "French and Indian War Diary of Benjamin Glasier of Ipswich, 1758-1760," Essex Institute, Historical Collections, vol. 86 (January 1950), 73.
[25] Sweat, 40-41.

Saratoga. On the fourth day, part of the troops marched the approximate five miles to Fort Miller, but others stayed at Fort Miller for only one or two hours. They then continued the additional eight miles arriving at Fort Edward, the main staging area for men and equipment heading to Lake George.

Two regiments deviated from this movement. Colonel Bagley's Regiment did not totally arrive in Albany until June 18, 1758 and then were ordered to head for German Flats on the Mohawk. Bagley's Regimental chaplain, Reverend John Cleaveland, expressed the dismay of the troops at this deviation away from the front. "My Regiment don't seem to be well pleased with our going to that place, but we'd rather have gone to Crown Point & Quebec."[26] Bagley's Regiment made it as far as Schenectady, about twelve miles west on the Mohawk River.

Colonel Joseph Williams' Regiment was also late to accumulate in Albany and did not march north until June 21, 1758 and arrived at Schenectady June 25, 1758.[27]

By June 23, 1758, Bagley had received orders that his regiment was to be replaced by Colonel Joseph Williams' on the Mohawk, and that Bagley's Regiment was to proceed up the Hudson River to join the rest of the army. The officers and soldiers of Bagley's Regiment were pleased by this turn around, and on June 24, 1758 his surgeon, Caleb Rea, wrote,

> "Last night Colonel received orders to march to Fort Edward, and Colonel Joseph Williams to take our station this way. It was said this counter march of ours was ordered because our Regiment had been recommended to ye General as better for a martial enterprise than Colonel Williams'."[28]

Colonel Bagley had served in the Lake George/Lake Champlain Corridor for the entire war, and his officer corps and many of his soldiers were veterans as well. Abercrombie wanted to

---

[26] "Journal of Reverend John Cleaveland, June 14, 1758 - October 25, 1758," Fort Ticonderoga Museum, Bulletin 10 (1959): 193.
[27] "A Journal of an Expedition Against Canaday By Moses Dorr Ensign of Capt Parkers Company Roxbury May 25th 1758," New York History, vol. XVI no. 4 (October 1935) 453-54.
[28] Rea, 97.

see to it that he had key players in his army. By June 29, 1758, Bagley's Regiment was at Fort Edward.

Now the Massachusetts men moved up the familiar "Military Road" from Fort Edward to Lake George, where the army camped, prepared their boats and launched for an all out attack on Fort Carillon. Around June 21, 1758 large numbers of carpenters moved up the road to Lake George, but some, like Benjamin Glasier were stationed at Halfway Brook Fort, a stockaded station between Fort Edward and the lake on a brook by the name of Halfway Brook. The men at both locations worked diligently on preparing whaleboats, bateaux for the flotilla as well as worked on defensive fortifications.

From June 24 through July 3 or 4, 1758 large groups, sometimes almost entire regiments or battalions of redcoats and provincials, marched the nineteen miles between Fort Edward and Lake George. The road was constantly congested with wagons, carts and units of men. Diarists list 500 to 5000 men on the road on most days. It was common to see 200 to 500 ox teams pulling artillery, whaleboats and bateaux, food, ammunition and military supplies on wagons and carts.[29] All the while soldiers built, repaired, fortified and trained.

Two basic types of training took place: basic military training, which encompassed the usage of their musket and other weapons, often called "military exercise." The second type of training was "bush fighting," more commonly known today as gorilla warfare. During the "military exercise" portion of the soldiers' training, there were numerous accidental shootings chronicled in diaries. On June 20, 1758, there were two shootings, one in the Massachusetts men and one in the redcoats. On June 22, 1758 a man of Bagley's Regiment accidentally fired his musket through the barracks at Schenectady, almost killing three men and a woman who was milking. Another of Bagley's men who was exercising his musket accidentally shot another of Bagley's soldiers, killing him and wounding a second. His musket was loaded with two balls, sometimes commonly done. The shots passed through fifteen to twenty men somehow not hitting them. A soldier of

---

[29] Cobb, 17; "Diary of Captain Asa Foster of Andover, Massachusetts," New England Historical and Genealogical Register, vol. 54 (April 1900) 183; Glasier, 74-75.

Colonel Doty's Regiment accidentally discharged his musket going through a man's belly, not killing him.[30]

During the build up of men, supplies and equipment and the construction of fortifications and preparations of a huge flotilla, there were several types of moral building taking place in the camps.

Each regiment of the Bay Colony, as well as other provincial and redcoat units alike, had attached a religious leader, their military chaplain. These men, almost always ordained, served on the regimental staffs. Their duties ranged from spiritual and moral teaching for the soldiers to seeing to the sick and wounded men's needs. There are numerous examples of preaching by the Bay Colony's Chaplains. Below is a list of some of the readings from their sermons of June 10 – July 2, 1758.[31]

> *Luke: 3.14* "Soldiers also asked him. 'And we, what shall we do?' And he said to them, 'rob no one by violence or by false accusation, and be content with your wages.'"
>
> *Deuteronomy: 23.12* "You shall have a place outside the camp and you shall go out to it, and you shall have a stick with your weapons; and when you sit down outside, you shall dig a hole with it, and turn back and cover up your excrement."
>
> *Deuteronomy: 23.9* "When you go forth against your enemies and are in camp, then you shall keep yourself from every evil thing. If there is among you any man who is not clean by reason of what chances to him by night, then he shall go outside the camp, he shall not come within the camp; but when evening comes on, he shall bathe himself in water, and when the sun is down, he may come within the camp."

---

[30] Cleaveland, 195; Cobb, 18; Foster, 183; Fuller, 8; Glasier, 74; Rea, 96-97; Richardson, 273.

[31] Cleaveland, 196-197; Fuller, 7; Holt, 307; Rea, 101; Richardson, 273.

Ezekiel: 25.12-17   "Thus says the Lord God: 'Because Edom acted revengefully against the house of Judah and has grievously offended in taking vengeance upon them,' therefore thus says the Lord God, 'I will stretch out my hand against Edom, and cut off from it man and beast; and I will make it desolate; from Teman even to Dedan they shall fall by the sword. And I will lay my vengeance upon Edom by the hand of my people Israel; and they shall do in Edom according to my anger and according to my wrath; and they shall know my vengeance,' says the Lord God. Thus says the Lord God: 'Because the Philistines acted revengefully and took vengeance with malice of heart to destroy in never-ending enmity;' therefore thus says the Lord God, 'behold, I will stretch out my hand against the Philistines, and I will cut off the Cherethites, and destroy the rest of the seacoast. I will execute great vengeance upon them with wrathful chastisements. Then they will know that I am the LORD, when I lay my vengeance upon them.'"

Mark: 3.8   "Jesus withdrew with his disciples to the sea, and a great multitude from Galilee followed; also from Judea and Jerusalem and Idumea and from beyond the Jordan and from about Tyre and Sidon a great multitude, hearing all that he did, came to him."

Judges: 20.25-28   "And Benjamin went against them out of Gibeah the second day, and felled to the ground eighteen thousand men of the people of Israel; all these were men who drew the sword. Then all the people of Israel, the whole army, went up and came to Bethel and wept; they sat there before the LORD, and fasted that day until evening, and offered burnt offerings and peace offerings before the LORD. And the people of

Israel inquired of the LORD, saying, 'shall we yet again go out to battle against our brethren the Benjaminites, or shall we cease?' And the LORD said, 'go up; for tomorrow I will give them into your hand.'"

Exodus: 17 "All the congregation of the people of Israel moved on from the wilderness of Sin by stages, according to the commandment of the Lord, and camped at Rephidim; but there was no water for the people to drink. Therefore the people found fault with Moses, and said, give us water to drink. And Moses said to them, why do you find fault with me? Why do you put the LORD to the proof? ..."

Ephesians: 6.18 "Put on the whole armor of God, that you may be able to stand against the wiles of the devil. For we are not contending against flesh and blood, but against the principalities, against the powers, against the world rulers of this present darkness, against the spiritual hosts of wickedness in the heavenly places. There fore take the whole armor of God, that you may be able to withstand in the evil day, and having done all, to stand. Stand therefore, having girded your loins with truth, and having put on the breastplate of righteousness, and having shod your feet with the equipment of the gospel of peace; above all taking the shield of faith, with which you can quench all the flaming darts of the evil one. And take the helmet of salvation, and the sword of the Spirit, which is the word of God. Pray at all times in the Spirit, with all prayer and supplication. To that end keep alert with all perseverance, making supplication for all the saints, and also for me, that utterance may be given me in opening my mouth boldly to proclaim the mystery of the gospel, for which I am an ambassador in chains; that I may declare it boldly, as I ought to speak."

One can easily read these biblical writings and look at the diaries at the events of the day and surrounding days to see the mind set in which the chaplain was selecting his doctrine. They start out several weeks prior to the departure for battle, lecturing the soldiers as to their cleanliness, their honesty and their daily lives. As it gets closer to the day of departure, however, the chaplains change their readings and sermons to reflect on the urgency of the task before them and attempt to prepare the men mentally and spiritually for battle.

The chaplains of the regiments saw fit to visit the commanding general the day before the army set out for Ticonderoga. Below is the description of the meeting.

> "Went to the General's tent and paid our compliments to him. Mr. Beckwith made a short speech or address to him in the name of the whole. He treated us very kindly, told us he hoped that we would teach ye people their duty and to be courageous, told us a story of a chaplain in Germany where he was that just before the action the chaplain told the soldiers that he had not time to say much and therefore all that he should say would be in these words, 'be courageous for the cowards would go to heaven.' The General treated us with a bowl of punch and a bottle of wine and then we took our leave."

Below is a list of many of the chaplains with the army.

> Rev. Forbush = Colonel Ruggles' Massachusetts
> Rev. E. Cleaveland = Colonel Preble's Massachusetts
> Rev. J. Cleaveland = Colonel Bagley's Massachusetts
> Rev. Woodbridge = Colonel W. Williams'
>   Massachusetts
> Rev. Morrill = Colonel Nichol's Massachusetts
> Rev. Ingersol = Connecticut
> Rev. Beckwith = Connecticut
> Rev. Cole = Connecticut
> Rev. Jonston = Connecticut
> Rev. Spence = New York

> Rev. Brainard = New Jersey
> Rev. Oglevie = Regulars

A second way of seeing to the soldiers esteem was the bringing of the regiments together to be reviewed by General Abercrombie and his second in command, Lord George Augustus Howe. This allowed the men to show off, so to speak, their uniformity, their dedication and their preparedness to venture forth and do battle against the French. Moral was most noticeably high when Lord Howe was present. He was not condescending to the colonist like many of his British counterparts. He took time to talk with them and learned the ways of warfare suited for the terrain of the forested North America. Howe had even ventured out with the famous ranger, Robert Rogers, learning the art of 'bush fighting.' Howe thought that light troops were the way to win the war.

By July 3, 1758, the stage was set and the Bay Colony troops were in place along with the rest of the provincial and redcoat army. Of the eight Massachusetts Regiments, Bagley's was the last to arrive at Lake George July 1, 1758. Colonel Joseph Williams' Regiment was poised at Schenectady to move west farther up the Mohawk River, and Colonel Ebenezer Nichol's Regiment was ordered to stay garrisoned at Fort Miller, Fort Edward and Halfway Brook. The time was right; the men and equipment were ready. An article from a Boston paper told it the best.

> "Boston July 3. By the latest Accounts from Albany we find everything is in a very promising way: __ That upward of 500 wagons are continually passing between Albany and the Lake: __ That 700 bateaux are built for the King's use, 14000 of which are already at the Lake, each capable of carrying twenty-five men, and their baggage, which is not great; neither officers nor men being allowed to carry more than what is just necessary; and that provisions have been got up for 25000 men for eight months."[32]

---

[32] Lucier, 92.

THE BATTLE OF TICONDEROGA

🍂 The Flotilla, July 5 🍂

On the morning of July 5, the army awoke around four. The weather was fair and the temperature was very comfortable for a July morning. The men ate a quick meal and struck their tents, carefully placing them and their few belongings into the boats. Each man had been issued five days food ration, which had been dressed (bread baked and meat boiled). The soldiers had been issued thirty-six rounds of powder and ball for ammunition as well. By five in the morning, the army began boarding their boats, and by six they had shoved off and were aligning themselves for the greatest flotilla in North America. There were just over 6000 redcoats and approximately 8000 provincials.

The flotilla was tremendous, over 1000 boats, 800 bateaux, 200 whaleboats and assorted barges, rafts and floating batteries. The advanced guard consisted of Rogers' Rangers on the left flank, Gage's Light Infantry on the right flank and Bradstreet's Armed Bateauxmen in the center, in 200 whaleboats. Each held twenty-two men. The main body of the army flotilla was made up of four divisions consisting of approximately 800 bateaux. Each bateau had five men manning oars and one with a paddle to steer. On the right were the Massachusetts Regiments, Ruggles', Preble's, Bagley's, W. Williams' and Doty's, along with New Jersey. The left division consisted of the Connecticut Regiments, New York and Rhode Island. The center two divisions were the redcoats consisting of the 1st Regiment of Foot, 27th Regiment of Foot, 42nd Regiment of Foot, 44th Regiment of Foot, 46th Regiment of Foot and the 55th Regiment of Foot. Following these four columns were the baggage, supplies and artillery in assorted boats ranging from bateaux, rafts, radeau (floating battery) and barges. The army's artillery train consisted of sixteen cannons, eleven mortars and thirteen howitzers. There were

160 bateaux loaded with ordnance and stores for the artillery alone, part of which contained 8000 artillery rounds. The rear guard of the massive flotilla was another Massachusetts Regiment, Colonel Oliver Partridge's Rangers. [33]

The splendor of this remarkable flotilla with a large red center and its vibrant, multi colored flanks, front and rear was astounding to the small town provincials. It stretched from shore to shore and at places about seven miles long.

The army rowed steadily north past the narrows of Lake George and about twenty miles up the lake. Then, almost at dusk, the army rowed ashore on a point of land on the west shore called Sabbath Day Point. Here they pitched some of their tents and placed guards. Some time between eleven p.m. and one a.m., one of the guards was alarmed. Some believe he was alarmed by a rattlesnake. The camp though, was mustered, boats reloaded and the flotilla again disembarked and rowed up north to the upper narrows where they held their position in the lake until the entire flotilla was together. Here they treaded water for the rest of the night.

---

[33] Cleaveland, 197; Cobb, 18; Fuller, 9; Glasier, 76; Hamilton, *Fort Ticonderoga*, 434, 436; Holt, 307; Lucier, 100.

❧ *The Landing, July 6* ☙

The flotilla advanced and orders were given to row up to the landing area where a hot confrontation was expected. About three miles out, Colonel Partridge's men were ordered to the front of the right column for the landing.[34]

A large encampment of French was spotted near the British proposed landing. Rogers' Rangers, the Bateauxmen, Gage's Lights with brigaded grenadiers and Partridge's Rangers headed up the advance. Rogers and his rangers were first on shore. They ran up to the French camp, sending the enemy to flight and killing four outright. The retreating French set fire to their blockhouse near the beach and left their tents and a vast array of provisions and liquors as they fled in a great hurry. Rogers' Rangers were sent after them and then scouted the area of the sawmills and secured the rising ground.

By afternoon, the British began to proceed into the woods to advance and attack the fort. The French had burned their bridges over the Chute River that ran between the two lakes, so the British were attempting to cross the river around the bend through the woods. Rogers had secured the area and built a temporary bridge.

Bagley's Regiment was at the lead of the Massachusetts Regiments on the right; Putnam's Rangers were in advance of the Connecticut regiments on the left; and Lord Howe, with his light infantry, lead the redcoats in the center. Rogers was successful in his mission, and Colonel Fitch's and Colonel Lyman's Connecticut troops were sent forward to support Rogers. About two miles into the woods the left column or wing was fired on.

A French guard had been watching the advance and landed by the British from Mount Pelee (Bald Mountain) at the head of

---

[34] "Oliver Partridge letter to wife, July/12/1758," Israel Williams Papers, Microfilm P-138, 1 real, Massachusetts Historical Society.

Lake George. Their commander, Sieur de Trepezec, attempting to get his men back to Fort Carillon, had surprised himself and the British left wing when he ran into them in the thick forest.

The first firing was reported to have been behind Lyman's Regiment. Portions of the advanced guard of all the columns and Rogers' Rangers began to respond quickly to the firing. Lyman immediately formed a front to oppose the enemy, Rogers rushed forward to form his left, and Bagley was ordered forward to move his regiment left and create a right flank. The firing was now between Putnam and Lyman. Lord Howe, rushing quicker than the other regiments, drove forward toward the firing with great haste at the head of the light infantry. Before the army's front and flanks could fully form, Lord Howe reached the firing at the crest of a small hill and was instantly struck in the left breast by a musket ball, throwing him backwards and killing him by piercing his lung and heart and shattering his backbone.[35]

By this time, many of the regiments were now reforming, and Bagley's Regiment was ordered to charge forth and run up on the enemy. Contact was made and a smart battle ensued. Bagley's men drove the French so hard that part of the enemy was pushed into the lake, some even jumping to their death from steep cliffs.[36]

Dr. Caleb Rea of Colonel Jonathan Bagley's Massachusetts Regiment tells of the din of the short but violent battle. "Ye heat of battle lasted but 6 or 8 minutes, in which time there was near as many Thousand Guns fired, which made a most terrible roaring in the woods."[37]

It is estimated that in this battle the French lost several hundred and approximately 150-180 were taken prisoners, but it is believed that the British suffered the greatest loss in that of Lord Howe. He had been the backbone of the expedition, the friend of all soldiers and the officer all looked up to. Abercrombie had been the commanding general of who made the plans, but Lord Howe was going to be the man to see that it was successful.

---

[35] Cleaveland, 198; Cobb, 18-19; Estabrooks 7\6\1758; Fuller, 9-10; Glasier, 76; Partridge letter 7/12/58; Rea, 102-103.
[36] Cleaveland, 198; Brenton C. Kemmer, *Redcoats, Yankees and Allies (*Bowie, MD.: Heritage Books, Inc., 1998) 6-7, *26;* Kemmer, *Freemen, 5;* Rea, 103.
[37] Rea, 103.

With all in confusion and darkness advancing, General Abercrombie gave orders for scouts to continue to look over the area for a march the next day, and all others were to return to the landing and prepare for another day.   Colonel Thomas Gage, commander of the 80th Regiment assumed the army's second in command.

✤ *The Sawmills, July 7* ✤

On the morning of the seventh of July, Colonel Partridge and Lieutenant Colonel Bradstreet, with 1200 men, were ordered to scout the sawmills. The sawmills were a second line of defense the French had placed to slow down an attacking army. Massachusetts Colonel Oliver Partridge explains what happened.

> "We soon laid a bridge over the lake at the falls. I marched to the French encampment where they had spread dissolution, destroying everything in their power. We progressed on with 3 Mass Regiments, My Battalion & Colonel Bradstreet with the Bateauxmen to the French advanced post within a mile of Ticonderoga fort, where here Montcalm was posted with 6 battalions. This place is ... of any difficulty to obtain before we come to Ticonderoga fort. Here they had a large entrenchment, which they destroyed & came off burning the very carts & attempting to burn the mill. After we had taken possession of this, the body of the army came up & encamped. Colonel Preble, Doty, Williams & I with our men were ordered to go halfway to the French Fort & encamp which we did."[38]

Abercrombie moved this day with caution. Not only did he send out scouts and a detachment to secure the sawmills, but also he sent out scouts to keep an eye on the enemy who were frantically working on some sort of outer works. Orders were given for the rest of the army to maintain better discipline and that no firings take place unwarranted. The army took their time advancing all day via the portage road leading from the French camp at the landing to the falls and the sawmills.

To secure their position at the sawmills, Abercrombie ordered a series of trenches and breastworks, one in front of the

---

[38] Partridge letter 7/12/58.

other. The closest one was almost within cannon shot of the French advanced guard. At least three brass cannons where placed in these breastworks.[39] In addition, two artillery pieces were placed on several barges and pontoons for use the next day.[40]

The majority of Abercrombie's army made it to the sawmills without loss. Here, they regrouped, were fed and those that could slept, spending an uneventful night attempting to rest. Some went into the sawmills wet and cold. Most of the Massachusetts men rested in their forward position, half way to the French fort.

---

[39] Cobb, 19; Rea 103.
[40] Pell, 36.

❧ *A Sorrowful Site to Behold, July 8* ❧

The British army arose early on the morning of July 8, 1758 and made their final preparations. The men were fed, ammunition was checked and battle plans were finalized.

General Abercrombie ordered a group of officers and rangers to ascertain his choice for attack. Senior engineer, Montressor, was ill. The next ranking engineer, Lieutenant Colonel Eyre, remained with the army. For unrecorded reasons, a junior engineer, Lieutenant Mathew Clerk, with several other officers, were escorted by rangers under the command of Captain John Stark of Rogers' Rangers. Their job was to reconnoiter Fort Carillon and her outer works. Around six in the morning, this party climbed the mountain, the English called Rattlesnake Hill, opposite the fort and across the Chute River. From this area they had an excellent view of the fort and the French working before the fort. Clerk and the other officers came back with reconnaissance stating that the defenses were not complete and they should be attacked immediately. Clerk and Stark also recommended that a battery of cannons be placed on the mountain they came from to cannonade the French works during the assault.

With this information General Abercrombie saw no warrant on bring up his artillery, including the battery recommended by his officers. His reconnoitering party had seen what they believed was an unfinished wall of log barely high enough to stand behind. Before these works was a crude abatis or obstacle of tree trunks and sharpened limbs placed towards an advancing enemy. Calling his senior officers together for a short Council of War, Abercrombie asked if they preferred attacking in three or four ranks. The majority of officers preferred three. Abercrombie ordered a frontal attack with muskets and the bayonet.

In actuality, the French had been working furiously on these entrenched lines. Approximately a half of a mile before Fort Carillon, a line of defenses was built. Here the peninsula was narrowed to about a quarter of a mile. The French left was flanked by a very steep slope down to the Chute River. Atop this position, the French had laid an abatis with six cannons to cover the flank. On the right flank of the lines was a portion of the entrenchments and troops. The center of the French lines consisted of logs laying one on top of the other. Some of these were up to three feet in diameter. The top of this wall was caped with sand bags. The wall was tall enough to hide most men except their heads, reaching six to seven feet high. This log wall was a staggered zigzag redoubt, which was an excellent apparatus for crossfire of their muskets and wall guns (small bore cannons). Before the wall, a short killing field had been cleared. All the tops of the trees that had been cut were carefully placed in an abatis or maze of sharpened limbs and sticks, an opposing obstacle to break the march or decimate the charge of the attacking British. The ground on which this was placed resembled a gradual sloping glacis.

By mid morning, the British were forming for their assault. At ten o'clock William Johnson and Captain Jacob of Major Rogers' Indian Company arrived with 450 natives. This contingent and a few rangers climbed to the top of the mountain opposite the fort on the other side of the Chute River and fired ineffectively at long distance all day. Also around ten in the morning, the French were driven out of their advanced breastworks.

At just after noon, Gage's Light Infantry (80th Regiment of Foot), Rogers' Rangers and Bradstreet's Bateauxmen and Partridge's Rangers advanced towards the French lines. Rogers' men were in advance and shortly engaged an enemy party. Quickly, the Light Infantry formed on his right and the Bateauxmen on his left. The French fell back behind their lines with the rest of their army. The British rangers and Lights advanced to the abatis and began a continual long-range fire.

The next lines of troops were the Bay Colony troops and the First New York Regiment. As these provincials came on line, the light troops before them aligned themselves also as follows. These regiments formed lines stretching from lake to lake. On the British right was Ruggles' regiment, then Doty's and before them was the British Light Infantry. In the center of the line next were Partridge's Battalion and Williams' Regiment. Before them were the armed Bateauxmen. On the British left flank were Bagley's Regiment and the First New York with Rogers' Rangers before them.

The battle plan was for this line of Bay Colony Troops and Yorkers to draw out the French from their lines. After three hours, the British Regulars were going to march in column between the provincial regiments and attack.[41]

As the army was forming, the only attempt of the use of artillery happened by the British. Several barges and pontoons loaded from the sawmills were sent down the Chute River in the hopes to rake flanking fire on the French left flank. One was loaded with two thirty-six pound cannons and the other with a thirty-six pounder and a howitzer. These were towed down the Chute River by bateaux. They were to be landed at the base of Rattlesnake Mountain and hauled to the top. This would allow artillery shells to be shot into the rear of the French entrenchments and also were to signal the frontal assault by the British infantry.

The British overshot their landing, putting their rafts within range of the French cannons at the fort that zeroed in on them. One was successfully struck by the French cannons, and the other was rendered useless and was towed back up the river out of range. Benjamin Glasier, a ship's carpenter from Massachusetts, took part in this attempt.

> "Eight day went up again and went to work to build two floating batteries for to carry the cannons on and the army marched forward and began to engage them about eleven o'clock, and they got four cannon on the battery and went down the lake so nigh the fort that they fired the cannons at them. So that they could not go any further and were obliged to return back."[43]

Before the regulars could advance a hot firing began on the left of the line, believed to be started by the New York Regiment. The provincials were drawn up closer and ordered to make a stand. The regulars threw down their packs, fixed bayonets and advanced in columns in good order.[42] This was not as ordered and the left wing surged forward before the center could form. This assault

---

[41] Partridge letter 7/12/58.
[43] Glasier, 76; Hamilton, 82; Lucier, 111.
[42] Fuller, 10.

went on for some time before the other parts of the army got on line and formed to attack using the formal plan. It can easily be assumed that the British advanced on the sound of the French fort's cannons firing on the British rafts, rather than the British cannon signal, consequently, the unplanned surge forward.

Once the army was aligned the British regulars sent forward two columns on the right wing between Ruggles' and Doty's Regiments. Next, British Regulars attacked in column between Partridge and Williams. Finally, a fourth column of British Regulars advanced between Bagley's and the New York Regiment. During these attacks the light troops and provincials kept up a continuous covering fire.

Around two in the afternoon, the British had been plunging forward with great vigor and fortitude, several times getting within feet of the enemy log wall. Seeing an opportunity, the French turned to deceit. Dr. Caleb Rea of Bagley's Regiment records the incident quite well.

> "When ye enemy saw the intrepidity of our troops, forcing the entrenchment with their bayonets, they retreated hoisting English colors thereby decoyed our men into ye French and then fired their cannon with small ball and grape shot slaying many hundreds, notwithstanding al this our men once and again got possession of different parts of ye entrenchment."[43]

By striking their own French flag, the enemy gave a moment's hesitation to the situation. They raised an English flag, giving the attacking British troops the idea that the wall had been breached and that they had brethren soldiers of King George within the walls. They rushed headlong into a massed barrage of musket and small cannon fire aimed at oblique angles at point blank rang. This was devastating and mortally hampered the attacking column.

For the remainder of the bloody afternoon, the British Regulars charged in columns, many to their death. The men of the Bay Colony remained in their formations, many taking what cover they could, and continued firing support to the charging redcoats.

---

[43] Rea, 105.

Most of these regiments were also engaged in building temporary breastworks for field defenses. Joseph Nichols, a soldier of Bagley's Regiment wrote in his diary, "Cut…down like grass. Our forces fell exceeding fast. It was surprising to me to think more of ye regiments should be drawn up to the breastwork for such slaughter."[44]

David Perry, a Massachusetts man serving in Colonel Preble's Regiment, told of his involvement. "They killed our men so fast, that we could not gain it. We got behind trees, logs and stumps, and covered ourselves as we could from the enemy's fire. The ground was strewed with the dead and dying."[45]

Archelaus Fuller of Colonel Bagley's Regiment chronicled what he related as "a sorrowful site to behold." "It held about eight hours. The dead men and wounded lay on the ground, the wounded having some of their legs and arms and other limbs broken, others shot through the body and very mortally wounded. To hear their cries and see their bodies lay in blood and the earth tremble with the fire of the small arms was as mournful as ever I saw."[46]

Several times, a handful of soldiers made it to the breastworks and it is believed that Captain John Campbell of the 42nd Regiment of Foot made it into the French lines to be bayoneted by the French. By dusk, a retreat was called, and the British began to fall back to the sawmills covered by fire from the rangers and light infantries until dark covered the earth. Confusion, fright and exhaustion now ruled.

Many of the troops made it back to the redoubt that was built the day before and the new breastwork built by Ruggles' Regiment earlier that day. Some men did not have the energy to make it far off the battlefield. All along the march of the retreating army were the moaning and groaning bodies of wounded comrades lying in their own blood, groping for help and grimacing in pain. Many of the men sat and fell down in exhaustion, some falling to sleep. Part of the Massachusetts men was ordered to hold their positions and wait for all the wounded and dead to be moved past

---

[44] Fred Anderson, Crucible of War (New York: Alfred A. Knopf, Random House, Inc., 2000) 244.
[45] "Recollections of an Old Soldier," Fort Ticonderoga Museum, Bulletin 14 #1 (1981): 6.
[46] Fuller, 11.

them down to the landing before continuing. In reality, many of the dead and wounded were left on the field.

Late at night, General Abercrombie ordered his officers brought together and gave orders to pull back to the landing with hopes of regrouping in the morning. Unfortunately, no one bothered to tell the soldiers the reason for falling back all the way to the landing, hence they assumed the enemy was launching a counterattack and the British army ran back to the bateaux. Joseph Nichols told the Bay Colony's side of the story.

> "News came that the enemy was coming to fall upon us. Oh the confusion we was in at that time for we was in a poor situation for an enemy to attack us, being joined to a point of land and the bateaux lay joining to one another fifteen deep from land. The cry of enemy made our people cry out and make sad lamentations. We made the best of our way off and received not hurt."[47]

The next morning, Abercrombie ordered all men on board the flotilla and the destruction of everything not in the boats. The army made a hasty retreat, making it all the way to the ruins of Fort William Henry before nightfall.

They left in such haste the French found much abandoned equipment, provisions, smoldering barges and pontoons, wounded soldiers and even shoes left by fleeing soldiers in the wet mucky places. Abercrombie's army was truly frightened. This was the most devastating day for the British Empire for decades to come: over 550 redcoats and provincials died and over 1300 were wounded.

In looking at the men that were wounded and killed at the Battle of Ticonderoga on July 8, 1758, there are records of four officers of the Bay Colony's Regiments being killed, one officer dying later of his wounds, ten soldiers being killed, and six officers sustaining wounds.

Colonel Preble's Regiment:
Captain Winslow – wounded

---

[47] Anderson, Crucible, 245.

Captain Goodwin – wounded
Lieutenant Macomber – wounded
Lieutenant Dorman – wounded
Lieutenant Adam – wounded
Colonel Bagley's Regiment:
Lieutenant Whipple – wounded (died later)
Lieutenant Burman – killed
Lieutenant Low – killed
10 private soldiers - killed
Colonel Partridge's Regiment:
Captain Willard – wounded
Captain Johnson – killed
Lieutenant Braggs - killed[48]

---

[48] Cleaveland, 198-199; Lucier, 114.

NABYCROMBY

The army arriving at the south end of Lake George was fearful, confused and exhausted at best. They had no idea why they had retreated but speculated that the French were or had already launched a counter attack. Many of the troops had now gone virtually five days without sleep, ate very spartan rations, and none stopped working or doing battle since July 5, 1758.

Many were stunned and mentally numb. Very little was accomplished as wounded men began to be transported south to the large hospital complex at Fort Edward. Unloading started but without much vigor. Hour by hour confusion mounted on July 10, 1758. Troops were told to ready the boats to head back to the north end of Lake George. Next they were to ready themselves to march to New York. Then they were hearing that orders were given to retreat to Fort Edward. After a Council of War was held by General Abercrombie, gossip circulated they were to make ready for a second attempt at Ticonderoga.[49]

The Massachusetts men were bewildered and criticized decisions of the retreat and the tactics of the attack of the French fort. On July 10, 1758, the Reverend John Cleaveland of Colonel Bagley's Massachusetts Regiment wrote, "This day everywhere I went I found people, officers and soldiers astonished that we left the French ground and lamenting the strange conduct of coming off."[50]

Dr. Caleb Rea of the same regiment criticized the tactics of the army.

> "The occasion of our precipitate retreat could not yet be discovered or why the enemy's trench was forced by small arms only when the cannon and mortars were just by and a whole day being spent without attacking the enemy at al which was time

---

[49] Fuller, 11; Rea, 106; Sweat, 44.
[50] Cleaveland, 200.

enough to have carried the cannon and laid a regular siege and it is remarkable that the greater part of the provincials knew nothing of the retreat."[51]

Lieutenant Colonel Artemas Ward of Massachusetts called the debacle a "shameful retreat."[52]

Colonel William Williams wrote to his uncle, "Leaving this place we went to capture, the best part of the army is unhinged. I have told you enough to make you sick, if the relation acts on you as the facts have on me."[53]

Others blamed General Abercrombie directly for the defeat. Colonel Oliver Partridge, commander of Partridge's Rangers out of Massachusetts despised Abercrombie. Many of the Massachusetts officers perceived the general's caution for cowardice. The provincials nicknamed Abercrombie 'Granny' and 'Nabycromby.'[54]

Lieutenant Elver of the 44th Regiment of Foot, a British regular officer, was very pointed in his opinion about the general.

> "Lieutenant Elver of the 44th told in my hearing today, his solid opinion was that the reason why the General ordered the retreat from Ticonderoga was his hearkening to Boys who never saw a fight and neglecting to ask council of knowing officers and that it was felt he never did ask council of any one experienced officer in the army."[55]

Captain Charles Lee of the same regiment went as far as saying that any blockhead should have been able to see the worth of utilizing the terrain better and implementing a fine artillery train.[56]

---

[51] Rea, 108.

[52] Anderson, Crucible, 247.

[53] Russell Bellico, <u>Sails and Steam in the Mountains, a Maritime and Military History of Lake George and Lake Champlain</u> (New York: Purple Mountain Press, 2001) 71.

[54] Anderson, Crusible, 241; Mason Wade, <u>Journal of Francis Parkman</u> (New York: Harper & Brothers Pub., 1947) 261, 337, 360.

[55] Cleaveland, 205.

[56] Anderson, Crusible, 247-48.

Massachusetts Dr. Rea blamed the lack of morals in the army for its defeat, but left himself a loophole if he wanted to revisit blame at a later date.

> "I can't but remark and that with regret, the horrid cursing and swearing there is in ye camp, more especially among ye regulars and as a moral cause I can't but charge our defeat on this sin which so much prevails even among ye chief commanders and those that were gasping for their last breath would commonly breathe out oaths and curses but as for ye politic cause I shall not at present give my opinion."[57]

Private Joseph Nichols arrived at similar sentiments as Dr. Rea stating, "we must submit for twos God's Holy will and pleasure."[58]

---

[57] Rea, 106-07.
[58] Anderson, Crusible, 247.

SECOND ATTEMPT OR HOME, THE LONG WAIT

Within a few days more unloading began and some assembly of a military camp emerged. Transportation between Fort Edward and Lake George increased, and General Abercrombie, though still very cautious, gave orders for the building of a new fort. On July 12, 1758, General Abercrombie and part of his officers laid out the fort on the rocky, uneven ground about a mile south of where Fort William Henry had stood. It overlooked the military road to Fort Edward and was very near where an entrenched camp had been in 1757.[59]

On July 13, 1758, two New York Regiments marched south leaving Lake George. On July 14, 1758, Colonel William Williams' Massachusetts Regiment, along with the Rhode Islanders and New Jersey men, were also ordered to march. This same day, orders were issued to stop work on the new fort and for the army to fortify by building a breastwork around the entire encampment. This continued for weeks. "Began to throw up a breastwork around entire encampment. Every regiment, regular and Provincial ordered by general to build their proportion in front of their parade," chronicled Samuel Cobb of Colonel Preble's Regiment.[60]

Work was a way to see to the safety of the army and the frontier as well as a way for General Abercrombie to maintain his cautious behaviors. It also put the idol hands of the worried soldiers to work in an attempt to reactivate army regimentation. Building projects instituted were the breastwork, a second fort, the

---

[59] Cleaveland, 200; Fuller, 11; Rea, 107.
[60] Cleaveland, 201; Cobb, 20; Fuller, 12; Glasier, 77; Rea, 108-109; Sweat, 44.

demolishing of the French siege lines of 1757, storehouses, hospitals, huts, sawmills, wharves and lake vessels.

Much of the building projects, including the shipbuilding, was orchestrated and carried out by men of the Bay Colony. General Abercrombie gave orders July 18, 1758 for the building of a vessel to guard the point. Overseeing her construction were Captain Joshua Loring, the Royal Navy Post commander from Hingham, Massachusetts, and Colonel Jonathan Bagley, commanding one of the Bay Colony Regiments in camp. The sloop was worked on by Captain Samuel Cobb, Benjamin Glasier and many other ships carpenters from Massachusetts until it was launched August 10, 1758. The sloop was named *The Earl of Halifax*. She made six expeditions on Lake George in the fall of 1758.[61]

By late August, 1758, the army appeared to be preparing to mobilize to, once again, cover the waters of Lake George with a mighty flotilla to attack the French Fort Carillon. On August 21, 1758, the carpenters of the army were ordered to parade and then to be sent home, but these orders were countermanded. Directions were given to the carpenters to build floating batteries and to repair all existing bateaux.[62] Two days later, Glasier and Captain Cobb were working with other ship's carpenters getting the proper timber for a forty feet long, fifteen feet wide row galley. It was to carry a twelve-pound cannon in her stern and mount five small bore cannons called swivel guns.[63]

In September there was still talk about the possibility of making another attempt at Fort Carillon, and to help out on this endeavor Captain Cobb talked about beginning work on a boat called a radeau. All through the month until October 7, 1758 men worked on caulking boats and launching new boats, including some large whaleboats that were being called bay boats.[64] Two radeau were constructed. One was fifty feet long and nineteen feet wide,

[61] Bellico, Sails and Steam, 71; ; Harrison Bird, Navies in the Mountains, The Battles on the Waves of Lake Champlain and Lake George, 1609-1814 (New York: Oxford University Press, 1962) 61; Henry L. Gipson, The Great War For The Empire, the Victorious Years, 1758-1760 (New York: Alfred A. Knopf, Inc.) vol. 7, 1949, 207; Francis Parkman Papers, vol. 42, p. 253-54, Massachusetts Historical Society, State Papers America & West Indies, vol. 87; Kemmer, Freeman, 51.
[62] Rea, 183.
[63] Cobb, 24; Glasier, 81.
[64] Cobb, 28; Sweat, 50, 52;

and the smaller was thirty feet long and seven feet wide.[65] These radeau were flat bottomed, seven sided floating gun boats with sides that inclined inward as high as or higher than a man to protect soldiers on deck. There were also gun ports along the sides to open and allow cannons to fire. They were truly floating fortresses.[66]

The men of the Bay Colony were not fairing well during the months after the Battle of Ticonderoga. Sickness progressed and became rampant in the camps. As the Reverend John Cleaveland of Colonel Jonathan Bagley's Massachusetts Regiment wrote in his journal, "people begin to sicken, partly because they were scared, and nothing to drink but lake water, and partly discouragement from disappointment."[67] The surgeon of the same regiment also stated, "Diarrhea and dysentery prevails much."[68] Less than a week later, on July 14, 1758, Captain Sweat of the Bay Colony recorded, "Our army now began to be very sickly and died very fast."[69]

The illnesses of the men in camp are chronicled all through the Massachusetts diaries. Men were sick from constant stomach ailments like bloody purges, diarrhea and severe dysentery, body aches and fever. Small pox, one of the worst communicable diseases of the colonial period, became an epidemic in the close quarters of the camps.

To give an idea of the death rate within the Massachusetts Regiments, the Reverend John Cleaveland wrote in his journal the soldiers of Colonel Jonathan Bagley's Regiment that died at Lake George and Halfway Brook post, from August 10 through October 15, 1758.

> *"Aug. 10 Dellinno from Captain Moore's Co.*
> *14 Richard Osgood from Captain Taplin's Co.*
> *28 Begalo from Captain Whitcomb's Co.*
> *29 David McDonald from Captain Whitney's Co.*
> *Gasper Macoouse from Captain Gidding's Co.*
> *31 Atherton from Captain Whitney's Co.*
> *Sept. 2 David Lunt from Captain George's Co.*

---

[65] Bellico, Sails and Steam, 75.
[66] Kemmer "Lost Radeau," Smoke & Fire Magazine; "The Lost Radeau" DVD Pepe Productions Glens Falls, NY www.pepeproductions.com.
[67] Cleaveland, 200.
[68] Rea, 107.
[69] Sweat, 44.

> 7   *Darius Hudson from Captain Whitcomb's Co.*
> 16 *John Duty from Captain Newhall's Co.*
>   *Josiah Day from Captain Gidding's Co.*
> 17 *Hugh Gordon from Captain Moore's Co.*
> 18 *Ebenezer Ransome from Captain Newhall's Co.*
> 21 *William Wise from Captain Whipple's Co.*
> 21   *Isaac Challis from Captain George's Co.*
>   *Ensign Bagley from Captain George's Co.*
>   *Corporal Dannel from Captain Whipple's Co.*
> 22 *Dudley Perkins from Captain Whipple's Co.*
>   *Henry Emerton from Captain Whipple's Co. (Halfway Brook)*
> 22 *Abner Ross from Captain Whipple's Co.*
> 29 *John Reed from Captain Whitney's Co.*

Oct.   *1 Hall from Captain Whitney's Co.*
> *Ring from Captain Gidding's Co.*
> 9   *Jonathan Wood from Captain Whiting's Co.*
> 13 *Nichols from Captain George's Co.*
> 14 *Jacob Smith from Captain Whitcomb's Co. "*[70]

Rations for the soldiers stationed between Fort Edward and Lake George had diminished to sub standard, causing part of the illness. Taken with many of the other things going on in camp and the stress, at least two almost entire Massachusetts Regiments deserted their post. On July 22, 1758, Colonel Oliver Partridge's Rangers marched away from their post.

> "The Regiment of Royal Hunters clubbed muskets and were marching out of ye camp by reason ye allowance of provision (which at this time was very mean through ye whole camp) had been detained one day or more but Colonel Preble persuaded them to stop (after they had marched near a mile) and he would see they had ye allowance immediately, which they had and returned."[71]

---

[70] Cleaveland, 204.
[71] Rea, 113.

Two days later, on July 24, 1758, at Halfmoon part of Colonel Doty's Regiment deserted. "Had advice from Halfmoon that Colonel Doty's Regiment being affronted by Captain Crookshanks a regular the great part deserted near or quite half ye Regiment."[72]

Within two weeks, the French and their Indians had begun to launch terrorist parties attacking the supply lines from Albany to Lake George. Early in the morning of July 20, 1758, an escort party of ten men marching from Lake George to Halfway Brook was ambushed. Nine were killed, one made his escape. Caleb Rea gives the most vivid report of the aftermath.

"Further advice from ye Halfway Brook assures us that ye action there yesterday was thus, ten men who was ye day before sent here to escort some wagons was on their return, and between six and seven o'clock in ye morning within two miles of that place they were fired upon by ye Indians and but one escaped, this exceedingly surprised the men within ye stockade so that it was with difficulty they rallied out an inconsiderable number and those immediately on receiving ye enemy's fire retreated or rather fled in ye greatest hurry and confusion save three or four of the brave officers ... who fought till ye enemy came up and knocked them in the head or cut their throats for several of them were found without a shot in their body anywhere."[73]

One week later, on July 27, 1758, another enemy party laid ambush and attacked a large convoy of military stores heading from Fort Edward to Halfway Brook destined for Lake George. Once again, Dr. Rea of Massachusetts Bay gave a unique telling of the story.

"This evening came in from Fort Edward a number of wagons with their escorts, they give us the following account of ye action near Fort Edward last

---

[72] Rea, 114.
[73] Rea, 112-113.

Friday ye 28 instant, viz.: that ye wagoners all made their escape save one, that there was 10, 12, or 14 women killed and missing, that ye escort consisted of about 150, that 40 were killed and missing, that ye teams consisted of 126 oxen of which 125 were killed and their horns taken off, one alive but his horns off, that they were loaded with ye richest camp stores but a most all destroyed, some say there was 30000 pounds sterling cash for bateauxmen and lost but others say there was but about 400 dollars in all, and chief or all belonged to private men."[74]

Major Robert Rogers, commander of Rogers' Rangers, was sent out with a party of approximately 700 men. They were to advance as far as Sabbath Day Point and cross Lake George to South Bay with the idea of cutting off the enemy's retreat. In this party were Rogers and some of the Rangers, Major Putnam and some of his Connecticut Rangers and some Connecticut volunteers, Colonel Partridge and his Massachusetts Rangers, Captain Giddings and a detachment of Massachusetts's volunteers from different Regiments, and Captain James Dalyell with a detachment of British Regular volunteers. Within the next week and a half, many other scouting parties were sent out from Fort Edward, Halfway Brook and Lake George with the hopes of finding enemy parties and partly because of false reconnaissance that a large French army was headed to attack either Fort Edward or the Lake George camp.

Rogers and his men progressed quickly north finding no signs of a large enemy party so crossed the lake and marched on to South Bay. Finding no enemy in retreat, Rogers' men headed back to the British advanced guard on an island in Lake George. Here on August 31, 1758, orders came in for Rogers to proceed to South Bay and then on to Fort Edward.

The party, according to orders, marched with little happening. On August 8, 1758, Rogers scout broke up camp and began their march to Fort Edward. They had chosen the area near the ruins of Old Fort Anne used in previous wars near the banks of Wood Creek. In the front guard marched Major Putnam and his

---

[74] Rea, 117.

Rangers. Following in the center were Captain Dalyell, Colonel Partridge and Captain Giddings and their men. Rogers and his Rangers were the rear guard. They were marching Indian (single) file. Rogers and at least one other officer, for unknown reasons, began firing at marks or birds. This warned a large enemy party in close vicinity who formed a u-shaped ambush. Putnam and his men marched into the ambush and received a heavy fire from the enemy. The surgeon of Colonel Bagley's Regiment, Caleb Rea, described the following in his journal.

> "This day had certain account of an engagement between ye enemy and our scouting party. Our commandants were Putnam and Rogers, who after they had passed up ye South Bay to Wood Creek and discovered nothing (it seems, at least Rogers party, grew careless, some firing at turkeys others at marks) they marched for Fort Edward, but ye enemy discovering them (as is supposed by their firing) ambushed them in form of a semi-circle which gave ye enemy a great advantage of our men. Putnam led ye van and Rogers brought up ye rear, and as they marched in Indian file they made a rank of a mile's length perhaps more. Putnam and his party only received ye enemy's fire and returned ye charge, for as soon as ye enemy perceived Rogers' party flanking upon them they retreated carrying off their dead and wounded what they could, our men pursued them not but took care of their dead and wounded and came off so that it seems rather a draw battle than either party victorious. Major Putnam missing and supposed to be killed but ye number of our lost is yet uncertain, as also ye enemy recovered by our men."[75]

Scouting and building continued vigorously at Lake George. Officers met, and men received gossip about another attack. One day, the men of Massachusetts received word that they were to pack and march home, but this was countermanded the same day.

---

[75] Rea, 181.

Another day, word came in of the capture of Fortress Louisbourg in Nova Scotia. Six thousand soldiers were promised from the Louisbourg expedition plus 10000 more provincials to augment Lake George's garrison to push again toward Carillon. By the end of the first week of September, Dr. Rea stated that men of Massachusetts were in a state of consternation about a second attack against Ticonderoga.[76]

On September 21, 1758, Captain Sweat believed that the Massachusetts men had only sixteen days until they marched home. All officers and men on furlough were called back to camp the next day. By September 24, the camp was again alarmed that they were not going home but against Ticonderoga. On October 6, General Amherst arrived at Lake George. He was the expedition commander of the Louisbourg attack and had arrived with his regulars. Amherst had advanced under orders, leaving his troops in Albany. He reviewed the troops with Abercrombie, but more importantly to the men of Massachusetts, they talked about the likelihood of a second attack.[77]

General Amherst left on October 7, 1758. The diaries speak for themselves on the matter drawn up by Amherst and Abercrombie. "The new general has concluded not to go on to Ticonderoga this year."[78]

"General decided we are to go into winter quarters as soon as the artillery, boats, bateaux and baggage can be secured and carried off."[79] "Second campaign over and preparing for winter quarters; get bateaux and artillery to Fort Edward; not sure if will be disbanded in November; sick and mortality in camp quite abated."[80]

For the next two weeks, there was a massive influx of wagons and carts carrying out the Lake George camp boats, bateaux, artillery and store. Sick men were carried out by large numbers, and regiments begin to march south and were sent home. One of the final chores was the sinking of part of the fleet of boats and ships to be left at Lake George, so they were not taken or destroyed by the

---

[76] Glasier, 81; Kemmer, Freemen, Bagley Orderly book, 89-102; Rea, 184, 186, 188.

[77] Anonymous, 296; Cleaveland, 224, 228-229; Fuller, 16; Glasier, 85; Holt, 309; Rea, 193, 197, 199; Richardson, 289; Sweat, 50-53.

[78] Sweat, 53.

[79] Cleaveland, 229.

[80] John Cleaveland Papers. Microfilm, Essex Institute, Oct. 11 letter to Wife.

British without a guarding garrison through the winter. Captain Joshua Loring of the Royal Navy stationed at Lake George reported about 200 bateaux, 7 whaleboats, 3 row galleys, 1 radeau and the sloops being sunk. This would give the British a head start on the 1759 campaign.[81]

On October 16, 1758, the chaplains of the army who remained at Lake George departed. A week later, on Oct. 23, 1758, Colonel Preble's, Colonel Williams' and Colonel Nichol's Massachusetts Regiments marched south for home. Finally, on October 25, 1758, the last of the Bay Colony soldiers, Colonel Jonathan Bagley's Regiment, left Lake George at nine o'clock in the morning in a light rain and snow mix. They arrived at Fort Edward and continued for eight more days there, enduring rain and snow every day but one. Leaving Fort Edward on November 1, 1758, the last men of the Bay Colony were home by November 13. One hundred and seventy-seven days in the service of their King, their Colony, and their God.

"This is joyful tidings to our homesick men who are many, if not most."[82]

---

[81] Bellico, Sails and Steam, 76.
[82] Rea, 201.

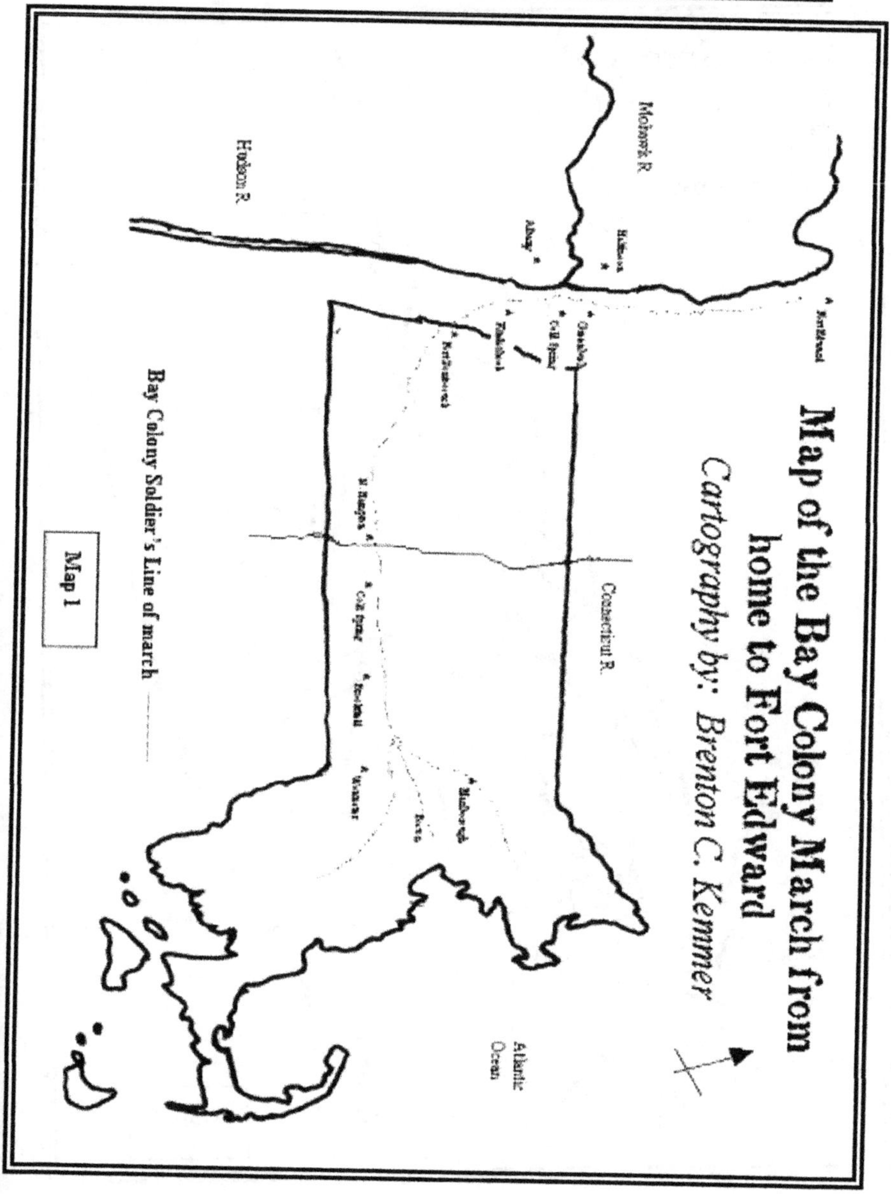
Map of the Bay Colony March from home to Fort Edward
Cartography by: Brenton C. Kemmer
Mohawk R.
Hudson R.
Connecticut R.
Atlantic Ocean
Bay Colony Soldier's Line of march
Map 1

Lake George / Lake Champlain Corridor

Cartography by:
Brenton C. Kemmer

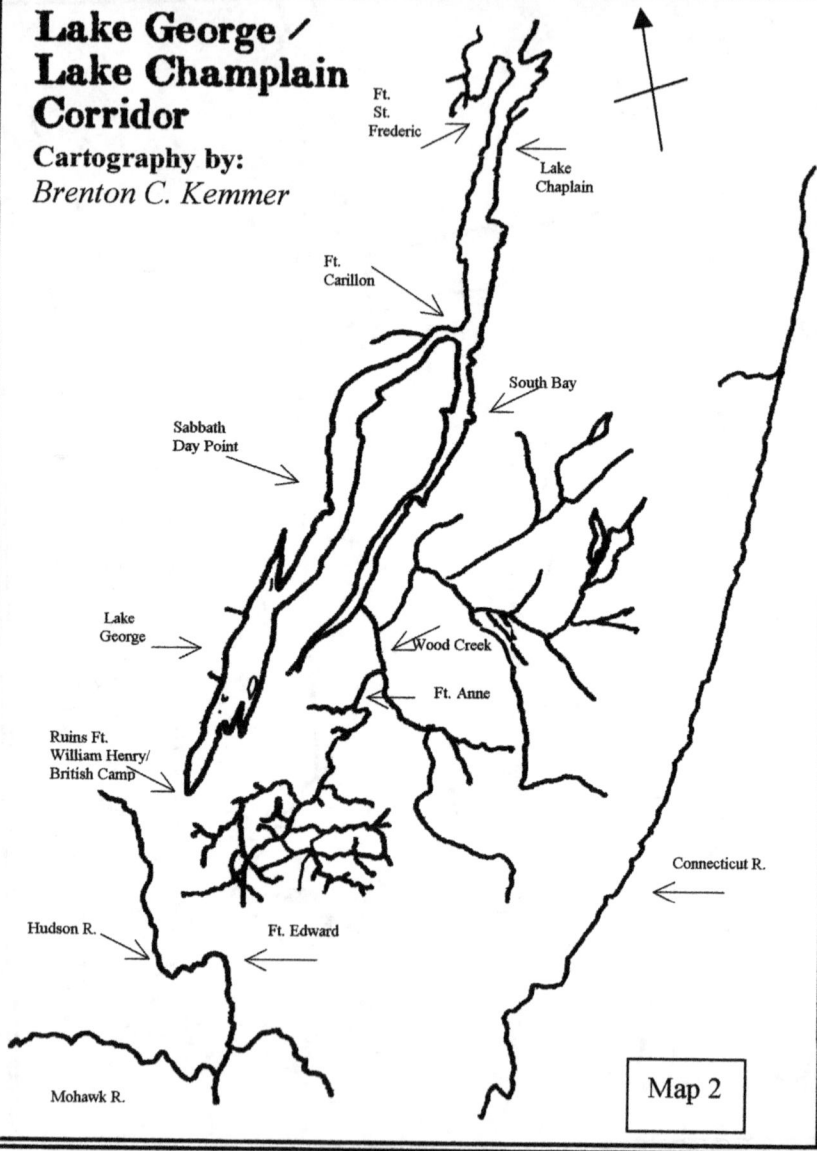

Ft. St. Frederic

Lake Chaplain

Ft. Carillon

South Bay

Sabbath Day Point

Lake George

Wood Creek

Ft. Anne

Ruins Ft. William Henry/ British Camp

Connecticut R.

Hudson R.

Ft. Edward

Mohawk R.

Map 2

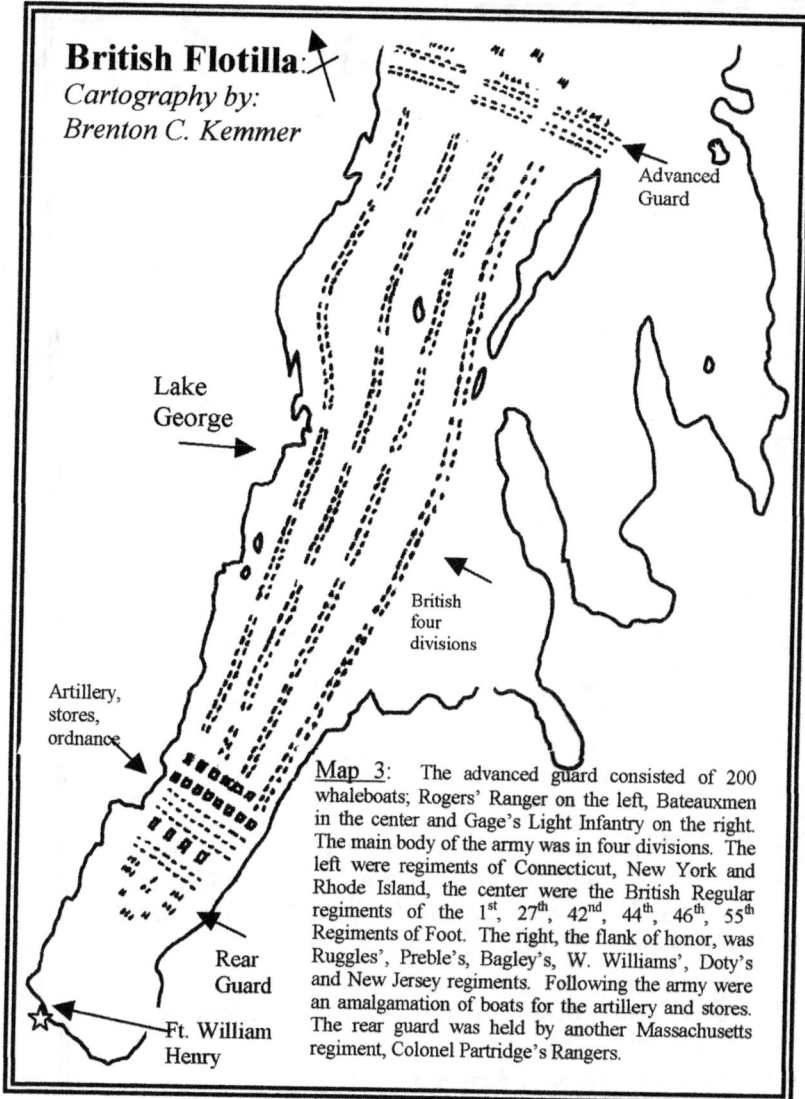

British Flotilla
Cartography by:
Brenton C. Kemmer

Advanced
Guard

Lake
George

British
four
divisions

Artillery,
stores,
ordnance

Rear
Guard

Ft. William
Henry

Map 3: The advanced guard consisted of 200 whaleboats; Rogers' Ranger on the left, Bateauxmen in the center and Gage's Light Infantry on the right. The main body of the army was in four divisions. The left were regiments of Connecticut, New York and Rhode Island, the center were the British Regular regiments of the 1st, 27th, 42nd, 44th, 46th, 55th Regiments of Foot. The right, the flank of honor, was Ruggles', Preble's, Bagley's, W. Williams', Doty's and New Jersey regiments. Following the army were an amalgamation of boats for the artillery and stores. The rear guard was held by another Massachusetts regiment, Colonel Partridge's Rangers.

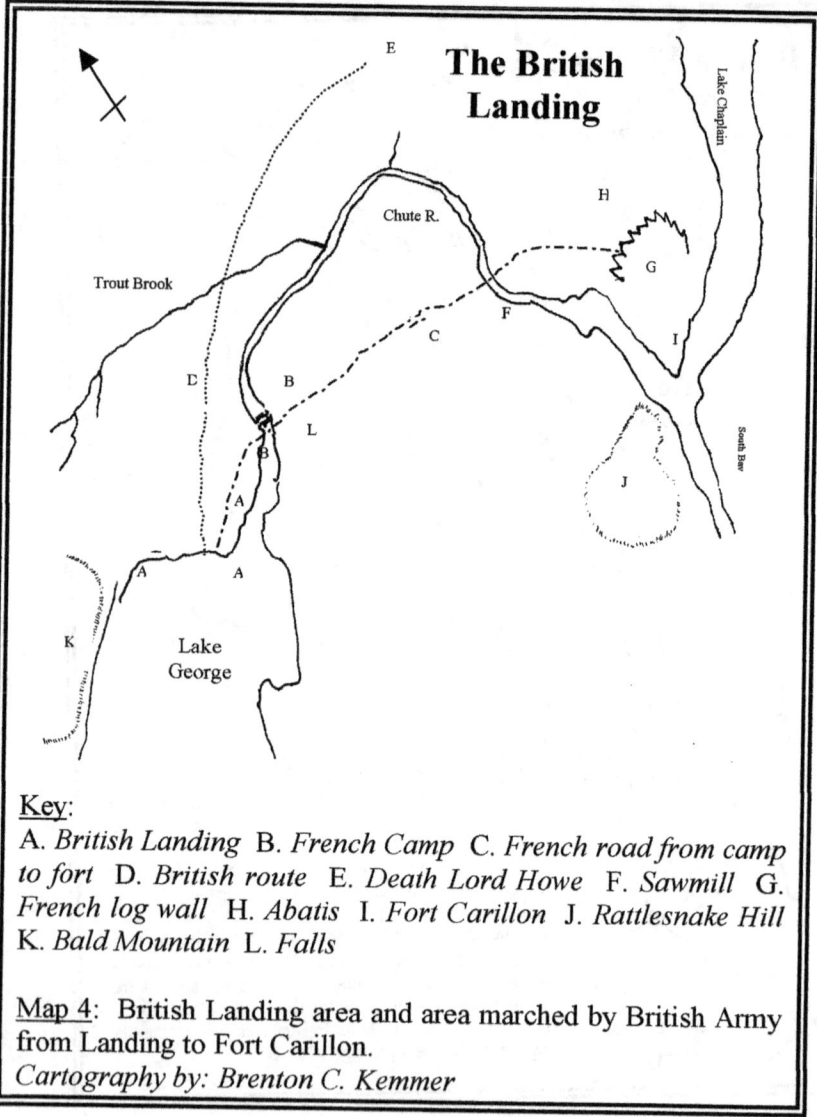

The British Landing

Key:
A. *British Landing* B. *French Camp* C. *French road from camp to fort* D. *British route* E. *Death Lord Howe* F. *Sawmill* G. *French log wall* H. *Abatis* I. *Fort Carillon* J. *Rattlesnake Hill* K. *Bald Mountain* L. *Falls*

Map 4: British Landing area and area marched by British Army from Landing to Fort Carillon.
Cartography by: Brenton C. Kemmer

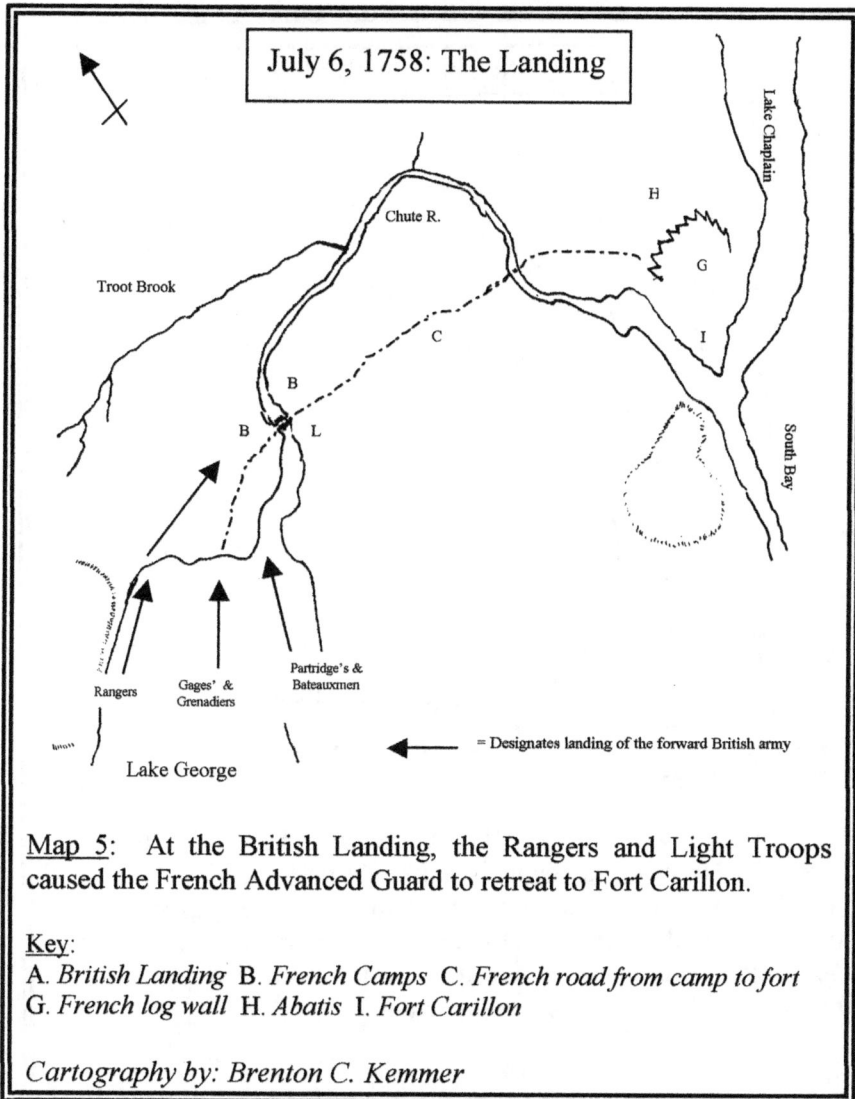

July 6, 1758: The Landing

Lake Champlain

Chute R.

Troot Brook

H

G

C

I

B

B   L

South Bay

Rangers

Gages' & Grenadiers

Partridge's & Bateauxmen

⬅ = Designates landing of the forward British army

Lake George

Map 5: At the British Landing, the Rangers and Light Troops caused the French Advanced Guard to retreat to Fort Carillon.

Key:
A. *British Landing* B. *French Camps* C. *French road from camp to fort*
G. *French log wall* H. *Abatis* I. *Fort Carillon*

Cartography by: Brenton C. Kemmer

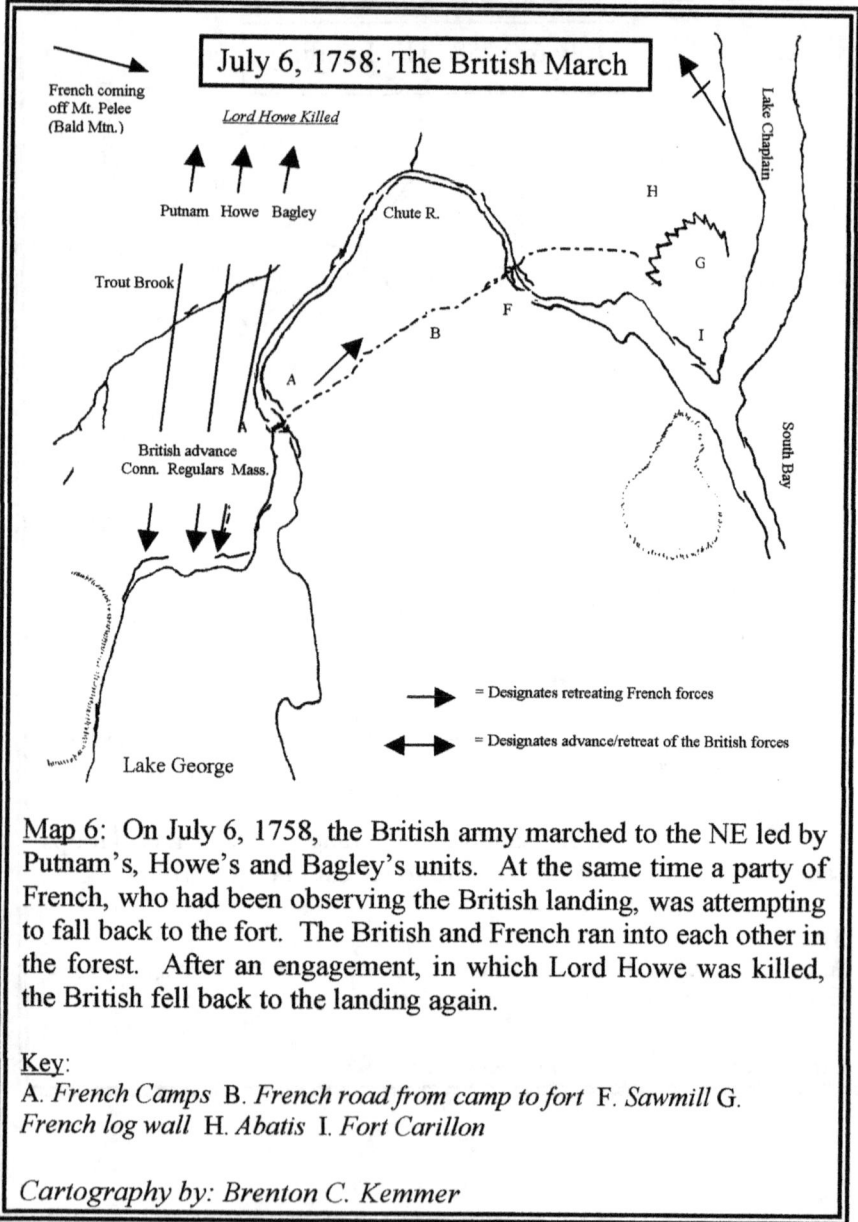

July 6, 1758: The British March

French coming off Mt. Pelee (Bald Mtn.)

Lord Howe Killed

Putnam   Howe   Bagley

Chute R.

Trout Brook

Lake Champlain

H

G

F

B

I

A

British advance
Conn. Regulars Mass.

South Bay

= Designates retreating French forces

= Designates advance/retreat of the British forces

Lake George

Map 6: On July 6, 1758, the British army marched to the NE led by Putnam's, Howe's and Bagley's units. At the same time a party of French, who had been observing the British landing, was attempting to fall back to the fort. The British and French ran into each other in the forest. After an engagement, in which Lord Howe was killed, the British fell back to the landing again.

Key:
A. *French Camps* B. *French road from camp to fort* F. *Sawmill* G. *French log wall* H. *Abatis* I. *Fort Carillon*

Cartography by: Brenton C. Kemmer

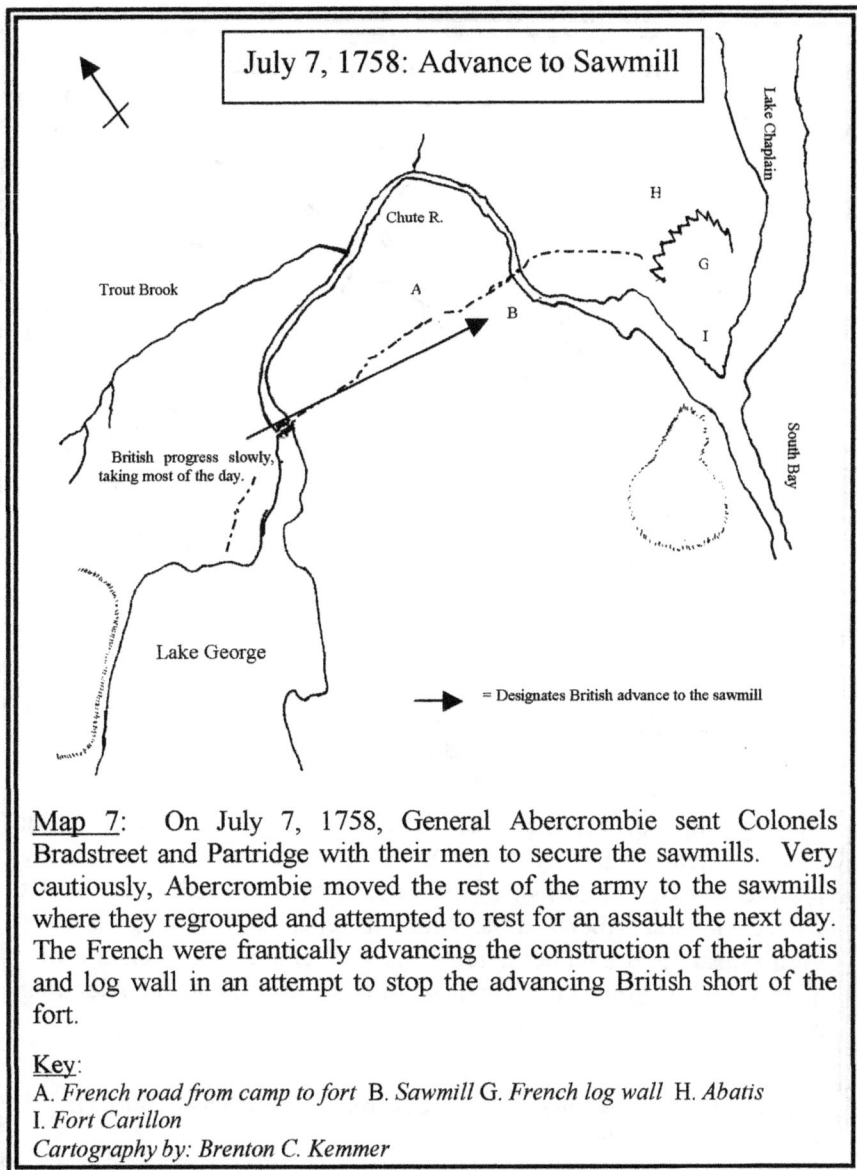

July 7, 1758: Advance to Sawmill

Map 7: On July 7, 1758, General Abercrombie sent Colonels Bradstreet and Partridge with their men to secure the sawmills. Very cautiously, Abercrombie moved the rest of the army to the sawmills where they regrouped and attempted to rest for an assault the next day. The French were frantically advancing the construction of their abatis and log wall in an attempt to stop the advancing British short of the fort.

Key:
A. *French road from camp to fort* B. *Sawmill* G. *French log wall* H. *Abatis*
I. *Fort Carillon*
Cartography by: Brenton C. Kemmer

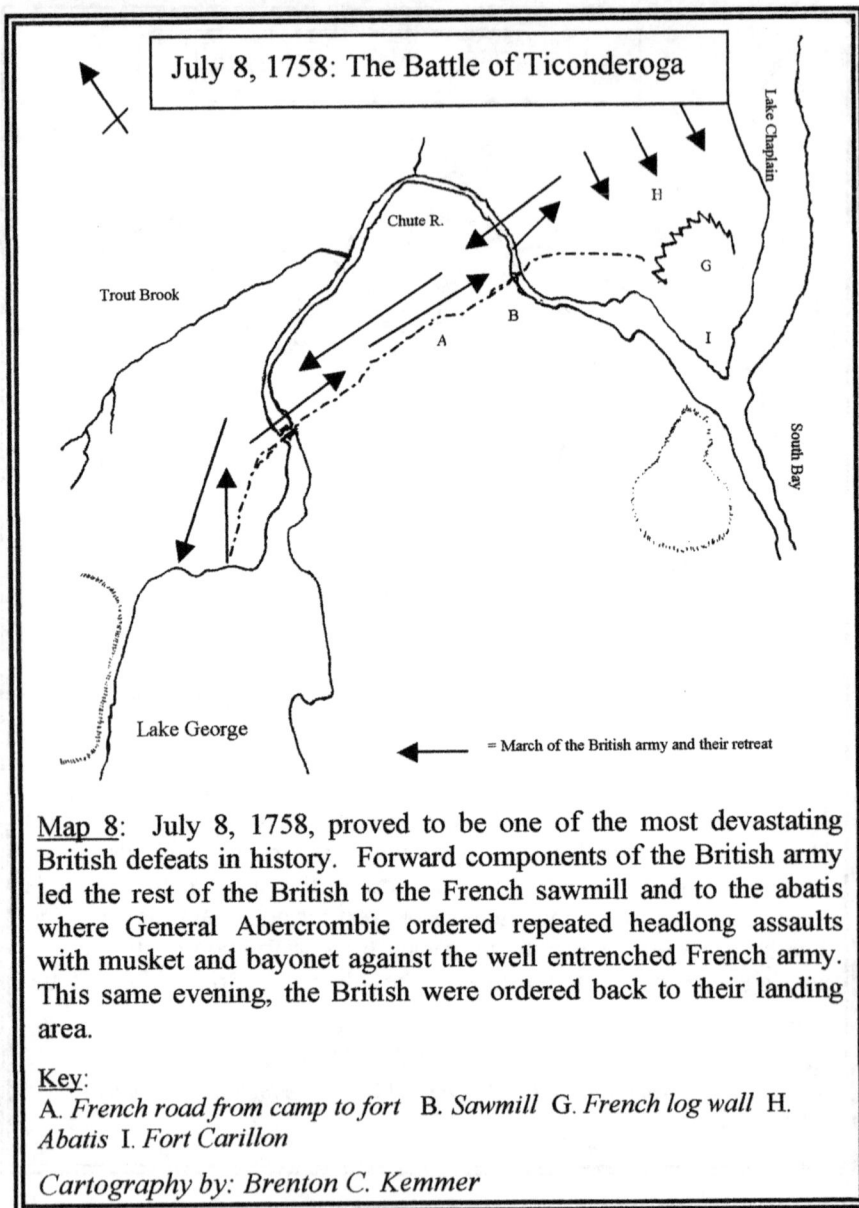

July 8, 1758: The Battle of Ticonderoga

Lake Chaplain

Chute R.

Trout Brook

H

G

B

A

I

South Bay

Lake George

⬅ = March of the British army and their retreat

<u>Map 8</u>: July 8, 1758, proved to be one of the most devastating British defeats in history. Forward components of the British army led the rest of the British to the French sawmill and to the abatis where General Abercrombie ordered repeated headlong assaults with musket and bayonet against the well entrenched French army. This same evening, the British were ordered back to their landing area.

<u>Key</u>:
A. *French road from camp to fort* B. *Sawmill* G. *French log wall* H. *Abatis* I. *Fort Carillon*

Cartography by: Brenton C. Kemmer

July 8, 1758: British Line of Battle at Log Wall

Key:
A=Rangers
B=Bateauxmen
C=Light Infantry
D=New York,
E=Bagley's
F=Williams'
G=Partridge's
H=Doty's
I=Ruggles'
J=Rear Guard
Connecticut & New
Jersey
K=British Regulars

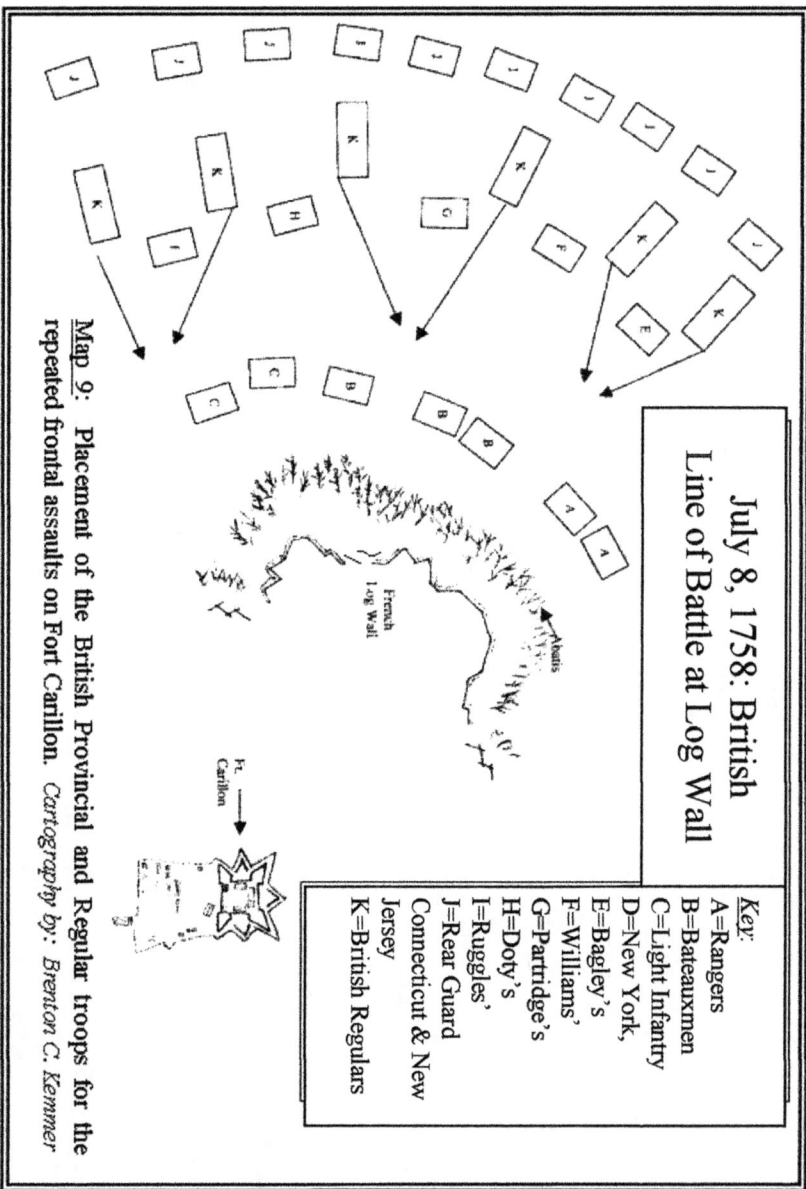

<u>Map 9</u>: Placement of the British Provincial and Regular troops for the repeated frontal assaults on Fort Carillon. *Cartography by: Brenton C. Kemmer*

Glossary

Abatis. – Gate or fence of sharpened sticks. Usually a horizontal post with sharpened sticks protruding to make an impassable fence work.

Artificer. – A skilled man. Usually a skilled tradesman in building in the military.

Bastion. – A part of the fortification usually on a corner that projects out in order to better defend.

Bateau. – French word for boat. In English military terms, a bateau was usually a double ended, flat-bottomed boat. Lengths varied according to usage.

Blockhouse. – A stand-alone fortified building.

Breastwork. – A temporary breast-high fortification. Made from earth, log, fascines (bundles of sticks), gabions (earth filled baskets), or other materials found on site.

Bush fighting. – The art of fighting in the woods. Utilizing the terrain of the forest. Sometimes called gorilla warfare.

Council of war. – A council of officers or the military family, used to help with military decisions.

Demilune. – A portion of the outer works of a fortification. Similar to a bastion with a crescent shaped ditch.

Entrenchment. – A trench work usually with a breastwork for added protection.

Floating battery. – A raft or vessel designed low in the water to transport and be used as a firing platform for artillery.

Glacis. – Part of a fortification. A gentle earthen slope falling away from a fort.

Harquebus. – A small caliber, smooth bore weapon utilizing a matchlock or wheel lock for firing.

Howitzer. – A large bore, short barreled cannon, typically mounted on a wheeled carriage. Shoots a projectile at high elevations. Commonly used to hit targets behind walls or entrenchments.

Mortar. - A cannon with a very short barrel in comparison to its bore. Primarily a stationary gun used to lob shells at high angles.

Parapet. – A defensive wall of a fortification.

Partisan warfare. – A type of warfare, specialized by light troops and rangers. Often involved in harassing an enemy utilizing gorilla warfare tactics.

Radeau. – A seven sided floating gun battery. This low-riding, flat bottomed boat was pointed on the bow forming a seven-sided polygon. It had sides high enough to cover soldiers and sailors within and was equipped with opening and closing gun ports.

Ramparts. – A mound of earth around a fortification, usually capped with a parapet, often of stone.

Ravelin. – A v-shaped outer work. Usually, between two bastions on a fortification's parapet.

Redoubt. – An outer work or a fortification. Separate from the other works and entirely enclosed to defend a position or point not defensible from the main fortification.

Row galley. – Sturdy gunboats moved by oars. These boats usually mounted a large bore cannon on their stern and small bore swivel guns on each side. Some reach sizes of forty feet in length.

Sloop. – Boat with one mast.

Swivel gun. – A small caliber cannon mounted on a swivel and used on boats, ships, and fortifications.

Trainband. – The colonial militias. Men of each colony belonged to, and trained in their militias monthly.

Wall guns. – Large bore guns, averaging 100 or more caliber used on the parapet of fortifications against infantry charges. Some were swivel guns, other were patterned after muskets, but a much larger scale. These guns were often mounted on swivels.

Whaleboat. – Double ended, round bottomed boat used for whaling. In the military this type of boat was used to carry primarily light troops and rangers because of its quickness compared to a bateau.

SELECTED IMPORTANT READINGS ON MASSACHUSETTS-BAY, 1758

Primary Documents

"A Petition by Ruth Farmer, wife of William of Whitney's Co. of Bagley's Regt., for reimbursement for his lost possessions in service in 1758, The Bulletin of the Fort Ticonderoga Museum, vol. II, July, #2, p.79, 1930.

Boston Prints and Print Makers, 1670-1775, "Officer's Commission for Joseph Ingersoll, 1758, Major of Bagley's Regt., promotion to Lt. Col. of a Regt.) a Conference held by Colonial Society of Massachusetts, April 1-2, 1971, University Press, Virginia, 1993.

Bray, George III, to Brenton C. Kemmer, 1993, Massachusetts Militia Exercise 1758, Photocopy, Kemmer Private Collections, Houghton Lake, Michigan.

"Diary of Nathaniel Knap of Newbury, 1758." Society of Colonial Wars in the Commonwealth of Massachusetts (1895) 1-42.

Gallup, Andrew, to Brenton C. Kemmer, 1994, "Part of, The Montresor Journals, G.D. Scull ed., Photocopy, Kemmer Private Collection, Houghton Lake, Michigan.

Hutchinson, Thomas. The History of the Colony of Massachusetts-Bay. vol. III, reprint London 1778, New York, Arno Press, A New York Times Company, 1972.

Journals of the House of Representatives of Massachusetts,
	Published by the Massachusetts Historical Society,
	Committee of Publication: Arthur Schlesinger, Robert
	Moody, Clifford Shipton, Walter Whitehill, Stewart
	Mitchell - Reprint of Journal of the Honourable House of
	Representatives of His Majesty's Province of the
	Massachusetts-Bay in New-England, Boston, N.E., Printed
	by Samuel Kneeland, Kemmer Private Notes, 1993,
	Kemmer Private Collection, Houghton Lake, Michigan.

Kemmer, Brenton C., "A Transcription of the Jonathan Bagley
	Orderly Book, 1758, from the Manuscript in the American
	Antiquarian Society of Worchester, Massachusetts, 1994,
	Kemmer Private Collections, Houghton Lake, Michigan.

Mason, Lt. Col. David, 1726-1794 Oil unknown artist, gift of S.
	Prescott Fay, 130,763, Peabody Essex Museum, Salem,
	Mass., Kemmer Research Notes 1995, and Black and White
	Photo by the Museum, Kemmer Private Collection,
	Houghton Lake, Michigan.

Massachusetts Historical Society, Boston. Seven Years' War
	Artifacts. Dispatch Box #0186, Cartridge Box #0428.01,
	Cartridge Belt #0428.02, Halberd #0249, Winslow Knap-
	sack #0946, Inspected, Researched, Photographed, and
	Drawn, Kemmer Notes, 1995, Kemmer Collections,
	Houghton Lake, Michigan.

Massachusetts Historical Society. Journal of the House of
	Representatives of Massachusetts. Boston: Massachusetts
	Historical Society, 1956.

Massachusetts Historical Society, Boston, "Victualing Records,
	Lake George, 1758," Artemas Ward Manuscript, vol. 2,
	Massachusetts Historical Society Photocopy, Kemmer
	Private Collection, Houghton Lake, Michigan.

Merrill, Joseph. History of Amesbury and Merrimac Massachusetts.
	reprint of Haverhill, Mass. 1880, Bowie, MD.: Heritage
	Books, Inc., 1978.

Mulligan, Robert E. Jr., ed. "Colonel Charles Clinton's Journal of His Campaign in New York July to Oct. 1758, During the French War." The Bulletin of the Fort Ticonderoga Museum. vol. XV, #4, Ticonderoga, N.Y.: Fort Ticonderoga Museum, 1992, p. 292-318.

Tonlinson, Abraham. The Military Journals of Two Private Soldiers, 1758-1775. New York: Books for Libraries Press, 1970.

Secondary Document

Adams, James T. Album of American History, Colonial Period. Chicago: Consolidated Book Publishers, 1954.

Amesbury Public Library Archives, 1995, Area Industries Through The Ages, Photocopy from Hawley Patten's copy, Aug. 27, 1976, Kemmer Collection, Houghton Lake, Michigan.

Amesbury Public Library Archives, 1995, 1884 map of Amesbury Ferry and Salisbury Point; Ferry District: As compiled from original notes of Joseph Merrill by Kathleen H. O'Brien; 1948 map of the town of Amesbury, Mass., Sketches of these maps showing the location of Col. Jonathan Bagley's wharf and ferry drawn by Brenton C. Kemmer, Kemmer Private Collections, Houghton Lake, Michigan.

Amesbury Public Library Archives, 1995, Leonard Johnson, Bagley Genealogy p. 24-31, donated September 1968, Photocopy, Kemmer Private Collection, Houghton Lake, Michigan.

Anderson, Fred. "A People's Army: Provincial Military Service in Massachusetts during the Seven Years' War." The William and Mary Quarterly. vol. XL, #4, Institute of Early American History and Culture, Williamsburg, VA., October 1983. p.499-527.

Anderson, Fred. A People's Army, Massachusetts Soldiers and Society in the Seven Year's War. New York: W.W. Norton and Col., 1984.

Anderson, Fred. Crucible of War, The Seven Years' War and the Fate of Empire in British North America 1754-1766. New York: Alfred A. Knopf, 2000.

Anderson, Fred. "Why Did Colonial New Englanders Make Bad Soldiers? Contractual Principles and Military Conduct during the Seven Years' War." The William and Mary Quarterly. vol. XXXVIII, #3, Institute of Early American History and Culture, Williamsburg, VA., July 1981, p. 395-417.

Anderson, Fred to Brenton C. Kemmer, 1994, Massachusetts Archival Records for Bagley Family, Kemmer Private Collections, Houghton Lake, Michigan.

Anderson, Martha and Norton Bagley. "Some Descendants of Orlando Bagley of Amesbury, Massachusetts," Genealogical Society of the Church of Jesus Christ of Latter-Day Saints. (microfilm, 1973) 1: 5-6, 14-16, 34-36.

Bellico, Russell P. Sails and Steam in the Mountains, a Maritime and Military History of Lake George and Lake Champlain. Fleischmanns, NY.: Purple Mountain Press, 2001.

Bird, Harrison. Navies in the Mountains, The Battles on the Waters of Lake Champlain and Lake George. New York: Oxford University Press, 1962.

Brooke, John L. The Heart of the Commonwealth, Society and Political Culture in Worcester County, Massachusetts. Amherst, Mass.: The University of Massachusetts Press, 1989.

Cardwell, M. John. "Mismanagement: The 1758 Expedition Against Carillon." The Bulletin of the Fort Ticonderoga Museum. vol. XV, #4, Ticonderoga, N.Y.: Fort Ticonderoga Museum, 1992, p. 236-291.

Coe, Michael D. The Line of Forts, Historic Archaeology on the Colonial Frontier of Massachusetts. London: University Press of New England, 2006.

Cuneo, John R. Robert Rogers of the Rangers. New York: Richardson & Steirman, 1987.

Currier, John J. History of Newbury Massachusetts, 1635-1902. Portsmouth, NH.: Peter E. Randall Publisher, 1984.

Field, Edward. The Colonial Tavern. Providence, RI.: Preston and Ronds, 1897; reprint, Bowie, Maryland: Heritage Books, Inc., 1989.

Fischer, David Hackett. Albion's Seed, Four British Folkways in America. vol. I, New York: Oxford University Press, 1989.

Flexner, James T. Mohawk Baronet, A Biography of Sir William Johnson. Syracuse, N.Y.: Syracuse University Press, 1979.

Frazier, Patrick. Mohicans of Stockbridge. Lincoln, Nebraska: University of Nebraska Press, 1992.

Gallup, Andrew. "Boats Used in the Lake Champlain Campaigns of 1758-1759." Journal of the Forces of Montcalm & Wolfe, Inc. vol. 3, # 2, April 1990, p. 12-18.

Gardner, John. "New England Boatbuilding in the 18th and 19th Centuries." New England Boatbuilding, Photocopy, p. 45-52.

Gaustad, Edwin S. A Religious History of America. New York: Harper & Row, Publishers, 1974.

Gipson, Henry Lawrence. The Great War For The Empire, the Victorious Years, 1758-1760. New York: Alfred A Knopf, Inc., vol. 7, 1949.

Hart, Albert Bushnell ed. Commonwealth History of Massachusetts. vol. 2, New York: Russell & Russell, 1966.

Hill, George C. Gen. Israel Putnam, A Biography. Boston: E.O. Libby and Co., 1858.

Hill, William H. Old Fort Edward Before 1800. Privately Printed, Fort Edward, N.Y. by the Author, 1929.

Hudson, Winthrop S. Religion in America. New York: Charles Scribner's Sons, 1973.

Hutchinson, Thomas. The History of the Colony of Massachusetts-Bay, From 1749-1774. London: John Murray, 1778; reprint. New York: Arno Press, 1972.

Jedrey, Christopher M. The World of John Cleaveland. New York: W.W. Norton & Co., 1979. Jennings, Francis. Empire of Fortune. New York: W.W. Norton and Co., 1988.

Kemmer, Brenton C. The Metamorphosed Soldiers of the French and Indian War. Bentley, Michigan: Cabin Craft, 1991.

Lawson, Cecil C.P. A History of the Uniforms of the British Army. vol. 2. London: Peter Davies, 1941.

Leach, Douglas Edward. Arms for Empire, A Military History of the British Colonies in North America, 1607-1763. New York: The Macmillan Company, 1973.

Leach, Douglas Edward. Roots of Conflict, British Armed Forces and Colonial Americans, 1677-1763. Chapel Hill: The University of North Carolina Press, 1986.

May, Robin. Wolfe's Army. London: Men at Arms, Osprey Publishing, 1974.

Palmer, Peter S. History of Lake Champlain 1609-1814. Fleischmanns, NY.: Purple Mountain Press, 1992.

Parkman, Francis. Montcalm and Wolfe. New York: Atheneum, 1984.

Peckham, Howard H. The Colonial Wars, 1689-1762. Chicago: The University of Chicago Press, 1964.

Perry, Arthur L. Origins in Williamstown. New York: Charles Scribner's Sons, 1894.

Redford, Sara Locke. History of Amesbury, Massachusetts. Amesbury, Mass.: Whittier Press, (autographed copy) 1968.

Rozell, Matthew A. Searching for the Hospital of Death, The Excavation of a Smallpox Hospital of the French and Indian War, 1757, Rogers Island, Fort Edward, N.Y. Fort Edward, N.Y.: Self Published, 1995.

Shy, John. James Abercromby and the Campaign of 1758. University of Vermont, Master of Arts thesis, June 1957, Unpublished, Photocopy, Kemmer Private Collection, Houghton Lake, Michigan.

Starbuck, Dr. David R. ed. Archaeology of the French and Indian War, Military Sites of the Hudson River, Lake George, and Lake Champlain Corridor. Queensbury, N.Y.: Adirondack Community College, 1995.

Starbuck, Dr. Davis R. ed. Archeology in Fort Edward. Queensbury, N.Y.: Adirondack Community College, 1995.

Stott, Earl and Jean. Exploring Rogers Island. Autographed copy, Fort Edward, N.Y.: Published by the Authors, 1986.

Stout, Harry S. The Divine Dramatist: George Whitefield and the Rise of Modern Evangelicalism. Grand Rapids, MI.: William B. Eerdmans Publishing Co., 1991.

The Colonial Society of Massachusetts. <u>Seafaring in Colonial Massachusetts</u>.   Boston: The   Colonial   Society   of Massachusetts, 1980.

Todish, Timothy J. and Zaboly, Gary S. <u>The Annotated and Illustrated Journals of Major Robert Rogers</u>. Fleischmanns, NY.: Purple Mountain Press, 2002.

Woodwell, Roland H. ed. <u>Maritime History of the Merrimac Shipbuilding</u>. Newburyport, MA.: Newburyport Press, Inc., 1964.

Zaboly, Gary S. <u>A True Ranger: The Life and Many Wars of Major Robert Rogers</u>.   Garden City Park, NY.: Royal Blockhouse, 2004.

Index